GoodFood

101 TEATIME TREATS

D1362611

10 9 8 7 6 5 4 3 2 1

Published in 2008 by BBC Books,
an imprint of Ebury Publishing
A Random House Group company

Copyright © Woodlands Books Ltd 2008
All photographs © BBC *Good Food*
magazine 2008
All recipes contained within this book first
appeared in BBC *Good Food* magazine.

All rights reserved. No part of this publication
may be reproduced, stored in a retrieval system,
or transmitted in any form or by any means,
electronic, mechanical, photocopying, recording
or otherwise, without the prior permission of the
copyright owner.

The Random House Group Limited
Reg. No. 954009

Addresses for companies within the Random
House Group can be found at
www.randomhouse.co.uk

A CIP catalogue record for this book is available
from the British Library.

The Random House Group Limited supports
The Forest Stewardship Council (FSC), the
leading international forest certification organization.
All our titles that are printed on Greenpeace
approved FSC certified paper carry the FSC logo.
Our paper procurement policy can be found at
www.rbooks.co.uk/environment

To buy books by your favourite authors and
register for offers visit www.rbooks.co.uk

Printed and bound by Firmengruppe APPL,
aprinta druck, Wemding, Germany
Colour origination by Dot Gradations Ltd, UK

Commissioning Editor: Lorna Russell
Project Editor: Laura Higginson
Designer: Annette Peppis
Production: David Brimble
Picture Researcher: Gabby Harrington

ISBN: 9781846075681

GoodFood

101 TEATIME TREATS
TRIPLE-TESTED RECIPES

Editor
Jane Hornby

Contents

Introduction

What's your ultimate teatime treat? A fresh buttered scone, or maybe a slice of rich fruit cake plundered from the tin? Whatever it is, you're sure to find something to suit your tastebuds in this little book packed with deliciously indulgent recipes from *Good Food* magazine.

We've got large cakes for a family-sized treat, as well as small cakes and tray bakes that are so simple they're ideal for getting the children involved. We know that most people like to mark seasonal events with cakes and cookies, so we've included lots of new recipes for Christmas, Easter, Hallowe'en and birthdays too.

If you're new to baking, or simply think you're too busy, I urge you to try one of our many recipes made in 30 minutes or less. You'll find that not only can home-baking be quick, but you'll also know exactly what's in each bite. There's plenty for keen bakers to get your teeth into too – perhaps you could craft your own brioche, or a fruit tart that could be straight from a French patisserie? Most importantly, no matter what your level of experience, you can be confident of success with every bake, as the *Good Food* team have tested (and enjoyed) each and every recipe. Happy baking!

Jane

Jane Hornby
Good Food magazine

Notes and conversion tables

NOTES ON THE RECIPES
• Eggs are large in the UK and Australia and extra large in America unless stated otherwise.
• Wash fresh produce before preparation.
• Recipes contain nutritional analyses for 'sugar', which means the total sugar content including all natural sugars in the ingredients unless otherwise stated.

OVEN TEMPERATURES

Gas	°C	Fan °C	°F	Oven temp.
¼	110	90	225	Very cool
½	120	100	250	Very cool
1	140	120	275	Cool or slow
2	150	130	300	Cool or slow
3	160	140	325	Warm
4	180	160	350	Moderate
5	190	170	375	Moderately hot
6	200	180	400	Fairly hot
7	220	200	425	Hot
8	230	210	450	Very hot
9	240	220	475	Very hot

APPROXIMATE WEIGHT CONVERSIONS
• All the recipes in this book list both imperial and metric measurements. Conversions are approximate and have been rounded up or down. Follow one set of measurements only; do not mix the two.
• Cup measurements, which are used by cooks in Australia and America, have not been listed here as they vary from ingredient to ingredient. Kitchen scales should be used to measure dry/solid ingredients.

SPOON MEASURES

Spoon measurements are level unless otherwise specified.

- 1 teaspoon (tsp) = 5ml
- 1 tablespoon (tbsp) = 15ml
- 1 Australian tablespoon = 20ml (cooks in Australia should measure 3 teaspoons where 1 tablespoon is specified in a recipe)

APPROXIMATE LIQUID CONVERSIONS

metric	imperial	AUS	US
50ml	2fl oz	¼ cup	¼ cup
125ml	4fl oz	½ cup	½ cup
175ml	6fl oz	¾ cup	¾ cup
225ml	8fl oz	1 cup	1 cup
300ml	10fl oz/½ pint	½ pint	1¼ cups
450ml	16fl oz	2 cups	2 cups/1 pint
600ml	20fl oz/1 pint	1 pint	2½ cups
1 litre	35fl oz/1¾ pints	1¾ pints	1 quart

There's no secret to making the perfect sandwich cake when you use this brilliant all-in-one recipe.

Classic Victoria sponge

200g/8oz caster sugar
200g/8oz butter, softened
4 eggs, beaten
200g/8oz self-raising flour
1 tsp baking powder
2 tbsp milk

FOR THE FILLING
100g/4oz butter, softened
140g/5oz icing sugar, sifted
drop of vanilla extract (optional)
340g jar good-quality strawberry jam
icing sugar, to decorate

Takes 30 minutes • Serves 10

1 Preheat the oven to 190°C/fan 170°C/gas 5. Butter and line two 20cm/8in sandwich tins. In a large bowl, beat all the cake ingredients together until you have a smooth, soft batter.

2 Divide the mixture between the tins, smooth the surface with a spatula or the back of a spoon, then bake for 25 minutes or until golden and the cake springs back when pressed. Turn out on to a wire rack and leave to cool completely.

3 To make the filling, beat the butter until creamy, then gradually beat in the icing sugar and vanilla extract, if using. Spread the buttercream over the top of one of the sponges, top with jam, then sandwich together with the second sponge. Dust the top with a little icing sugar before serving.

• Per slice 558 kcalories, protein 5g, carbohydrate 76g, fat 28g, saturated fat 17g, fibre 0.6g, added sugar 57g, salt 0.9g

An easy Middle-Eastern-style cake that uses a very British ingredient.

Bitter orange and poppy seed cake

3 tbsp good-quality thick-cut
marmalade
150g carton natural bio yogurt
3 eggs
175g/6oz golden caster sugar
200g/8oz self-raising flour
½ tsp baking powder
175g/6oz butter, softened
zest of 1 orange
2 tsp poppy seeds, toasted

FOR THE STICKY TOPPING
juice of ½ orange
5 tbsp good-quality thick-cut
marmalade

Takes 1 hour 15 minutes • Serves 8

1 Preheat the oven to 160°C/fan 140°C/
gas 3. Butter a 20x10cm/8x4in loaf tin and
line the base. Melt the marmalade in a pan,
beat in the yogurt and let it cool.
2 Whisk the remaining cake ingredients until
smooth. Quickly beat in the yogurt mix, then
pour the batter into the tin. Leave it mounded
in the centre to help it rise in the middle.
3 Bake for 1 hour or until golden and a
skewer inserted comes out clean. If the
cake has taken on a lot of colour after 45
minutes, loosely cover it with baking paper.
4 Meanwhile, melt the orange juice and
marmalade together. When the cake is ready,
cool in the tin for 10 minutes, then turn out on
to a wire rack. Once the cake is just warm,
spoon over the glaze.

• Per slice 422 kcalories, protein 6g, carbohydrate
54g, fat 21g, saturated fat 12g, fibre 1g, sugar 35g,
salt 0.80g

All the great flavours of Spain are combined in this easy cake.

Almond raisin cake with sherry

250g/9oz raisins
200ml/7fl oz medium or sweet sherry
(try amontillado or Pedro Ximénez)
150ml carton thick natural yogurt
150ml/5fl oz vegetable oil
3 eggs
140g/5oz plain flour
100g/4oz ground almonds
2 tsp baking powder
100g/4oz light muscovado sugar
icing sugar, to serve

Takes 1 hour 5 minutes, plus marinating
Serves 6, with leftovers

1 Tip the raisins into a bowl, pour over the sherry, then leave for 30 minutes. Preheat the oven to 180°C/fan 160°C/gas 4. Grease and line a 20cm/8in round cake tin.
2 Mix together the yogurt, oil and eggs. Put the dry ingredients into a large bowl, pour in the yogurt mixture, then mix until smooth. Scoop half the raisins out of the sherry and stir into the batter. Spoon into the tin and smooth the top with a spoon. Bake for 50–55 minutes or until springy and a skewer inserted into the middle of the cake comes out clean.
3 Once cooked, prick the cake with a skewer and spoon over five tablespoons of the sherry. Warm the rest of the soaked raisins and sherry to serve with the cake, warm or cool and dusted with icing sugar.

• Per slice 501 kcalories, protein 9g, carbohydrate 52g, fat 27g, saturated fat 4g, fibre 2g, sugar 38g, salt 0.57g

Wrapped in cellophane and tied with a festive ribbon, these gorgeous cakes make a great Christmas gift.

Cranberry pecan and ginger loaf

250g butter, chopped
250g/9oz light muscovado sugar
175g/6oz dried cranberries
175g/6oz dried apricots, chopped
zest and juice of 1 large orange
5 tbsp brandy
175g/6oz pecan halves (grind 100g/4oz of them)
300g/10oz plain flour
2 tsp baking powder
2 tsp ground ginger
1 tsp ground cinnamon
4 eggs, beaten
50g/2oz crystallized ginger, chopped

TO DECORATE
3 tbsp apricot jam, warmed then sieved
icing sugar, for dusting
250g block marzipan
extra nuts and dried fruit, to decorate

Takes 3–3½ hours • Makes two cakes, each of which serves 12–14

1 Preheat the oven to 150°C/fan 130°C/gas 2. Butter and double-line a 20cm/8in square tin. Put the butter, sugar, fruit, zest, juice and brandy into a pan. Bring slowly to the boil, stirring. Simmer for 10 minutes. Cool.
2 Thoroughly mix the dry ingredients, eggs and crystallized ginger into the pan. Spoon into the tin. Bake for 1 hour, then reduce to 140°C/fan 120°C/gas 1 and cook for 1½– 2 hours more, until firm and a skewer inserted into the centre comes out clean. Cool in the tin for 10 minutes. Turn out on to a wire rack.
3 Stir one tablespoon of water into the jam, then brush most of it over the cake. Lightly dust the surface with icing sugar, then top with a 20cm/8in square of marzipan. Trim the edges then cut the cake in half. Brush with remaining jam and decorate.

• Per slice (for 12) 347 kcalories, protein 4g, carbohydrate 42g, fat 18g, saturated fat 7g, fibre 2g, sugar 31g, salt 0.35g

If you've offered to bake a treat for a stall at a fair or for your local coffee morning, this version of a classic is just the thing.

Cappuccino cake

250g butter, softened
250g/9oz light brown soft sugar, plus 2–3 tbsp extra
300g/10oz self-raising flour
4 eggs, beaten
50g/2oz walnut halves, toasted and finely chopped – using a food processor is easiest
200ml/7fl oz very strong coffee (fresh or instant), cooled

FOR THE FROSTING
500g carton mascarpone
2 tbsp light brown soft sugar
cocoa powder or drinking chocolate, to decorate

Takes 45 minutes • Serves 12

1 Preheat the oven to 180°C/fan 160°C/gas 4. Butter and line the bottoms of two 20cm/8in sandwich tins with greaseproof paper. Beat the butter and sugar together with electric beaters until pale. Add the flour and eggs and keep beating until evenly mixed. Fold in the walnuts and half of the coffee. Spoon into the prepared tins and bake for 25–30 minutes or until golden and well risen. Leave in their tins for 5 minutes before cooling on a wire rack.
2 Sweeten the rest of the coffee with the extra sugar and drizzle four tablespoons over the sponges. Leave to cool completely.
3 For the frosting, beat the mascarpone, sugar and remaining coffee until smooth. Use half of the frosting to sandwich the sponges together. Spread the rest over the top of the cake. Decorate with a dusting of cocoa powder.

• Per slice 559 kcalories, protein 5g, carbohydrate 48g, fat 39g, saturated fat 23g, fibre 1g, added sugar 29g, salt 0.72g

This delicious family favourite is made even tastier by the addition of tangy orange juice and a delicious cream cheese frosting.

Carrot cake loaf with vanilla frosting

85g/3oz sultanas
juice of 1 orange
85g/3oz wholemeal flour
85g/3oz self-raising flour
175g/6oz light brown soft sugar
1 tsp bicarbonate of soda
1 tsp ground cinnamon
1 tsp mixed spice
½ tsp salt
125ml/4fl oz sunflower oil, plus extra for greasing
2 eggs, beaten
175g/6oz carrots, peeled and coarsely grated (about 2 large carrots)
50g/2oz walnut halves, roughly chopped, plus extra to decorate

FOR THE FROSTING
85g/3oz full-fat soft cheese
25g/1oz butter, softened
1 tsp vanilla extract
175g/6oz icing sugar, sifted

Takes 1 hour 20 minutes • Serves 10

1 Soak the sultanas in the orange juice for 3–4 hours or overnight. Preheat the oven to 180°C/fan 160°C/gas 4. Grease and line a 900g/2lb loaf tin. Sift the flours, sugar, bicarbonate of soda, spices and salt into a large bowl. Pour in the oil and eggs, and mix well, then fold in the carrots, walnuts and the sultanas with their orange juice.
2 Spoon the mixture into the tin then bake for 1 hour or until firm and a skewer inserted comes out clean. Cool for a few minutes, then turn out of the tin on to a wire rack.
3 Beat the soft cheese, butter, vanilla and icing sugar until smooth, and chill until needed. When cool, split the cake in half, spread the bottom with half of the frosting. Replace the top, then swirl over the remaining frosting. Decorate with walnuts.

• Per slice 422 kcalories, protein 5g, carbohydrate 57g, fat 21g, saturated fat 5g, fibre 2g, sugar 45g, salt 0.88g

Large and loaf cakes

If you like lemon drizzle, you'll love this easy loaf.

Sticky lime and coconut drizzle loaf

100g/4oz butter, softened
175g/6oz self-raising flour
1 tsp baking powder
175g/6oz golden caster sugar
2 eggs
½ × 400ml can coconut milk
finely grated zest of 2 limes

FOR THE ICING AND TO DECORATE
½ × 400ml can coconut milk
200g/8oz golden caster sugar
finely grated zest of 1 lime
juice of the 3 limes

Takes 1 hour 5 minutes • Serves 10

1 Preheat the oven to 180°C/fan 160°C/ gas 4. Butter and line a 900g/2lb loaf tin with baking parchment. Beat all the cake ingredients together until combined. Tip into the tin and smooth the top. Bake for 40 minutes, until golden and firm to touch.
2 For the icing, tip the coconut milk and 150g/5½oz of the sugar into a pan. Boil for 5 minutes or until syrupy (so you can see the bottom of the pan when you stir). Stir in the lime juice. Set aside. Mix the remaining sugar and lime zest to a paste, then set aside.
3 Leave the cooked loaf in the tin while you pour over the icing a little at a time – wait for the cake to absorb it before adding more. Cool, then carefully remove from the tin, sprinkle with the lime sugar and slice.

• Per slice 364 kcalories, protein 4g, carbohydrate 54g, fat 16g, saturated fat 11g, fibre 1g, sugar 41g, salt 0.62g

This cake is wonderfully light and nutty and is great served warm as a dessert or cut into thin slices for tea.

Italian hazelnut cake

200g bag blanched hazelnuts
5 eggs
175g/6oz caster sugar
100g/4oz butter, melted
1 tsp vanilla extract
icing sugar, for dusting

Takes 1 hour 10–20 minutes • Serves 8

1 Preheat the oven to 180°C/fan 160°C/ gas 4. Butter and line the base of a deep 20cm/8in round cake tin. Grind the hazelnuts in a food processor or blender until they are as fine as you can get them. If they seem damp, spread them out on a baking sheet to dry for half an hour or so, stirring occasionally.
2 Separate the eggs into two large bowls. Tip the sugar on to the yolks and use an electric beater for about 3 minutes or until the mixture leaves a trail on the surface when the whisk blades are lifted. Gradually whisk in the melted butter, then fold in the hazelnuts and vanilla.
3 Using clean blades, whisk the egg whites until stiff, then fold into the cake mixture in four equal batches. Pour into the tin and bake for 50–60 minutes or until firm but springy. Cool in the tin for 10 minutes, then turn out and leave to cool. Dust with icing sugar.

• Per slice 394 kcalories, protein 9.7g, carbohydrate 54.3g, fat 17g, saturated fat 14g, fibre 4g, added sugar none, salt 1g

Citrus syrup makes this cake wonderfully moist and elevates it from a simple teatime bake to a delicious dinner-party dessert.

Orange and saffron syrup cake

100g/4oz hazelnuts, skinned and ground
50g/2oz semolina or polenta
175g/6oz golden caster sugar
1½ tsp baking powder
2 large oranges
4 medium eggs
200ml/7fl oz light olive oil
generous pinch of saffron threads
85g/3oz icing sugar
Greek yogurt or crème fraîche and orange segments, to serve (optional)

Takes about 1 hour • Serves 8

1 Preheat the oven to 180°C/fan 160°C/gas 4. Oil the base of a 23cm/9in ring tin. Put the ground hazelnuts in a frying pan and toast over a medium heat, stirring frequently until evenly browned. Cool, then mix with the semolina, caster sugar and baking powder.
2 Beat the zest of one orange with the eggs and oil, then fold into the semolina mix. Pour into the tin and bake for 30–40 minutes or until risen and firm to the touch.
3 While the cake is baking, pare the zest from the other orange and cut it into very thin shreds. Put into a pan with the juice of both oranges, the saffron and icing sugar. Bring to the boil, then simmer gently for 5 minutes.
4 Leave the cake to cool slightly then turn out on to a plate. While the cake is still warm, skewer it and spoon over the orange and saffron syrup. Serve with Greek yogurt.

• Per slice 455 kcalories, protein 7g, carbohydrate 43g, fat 30g, saturated fat 4g, fibre 2g, added sugar 33g, salt 0.4g

This cake improves with keeping – if it lasts that long! It is much easier to grate root ginger from frozen, so store a chunk in a bag in the freezer until needed.

Squidgy lemon–ginger cake

200g/8oz dates, stoned
200g/8oz butter, cubed
300g/10oz dark muscovado sugar
2 eggs
50g/2oz fresh or frozen root ginger, grated
grated zest of 1 lemon
200g/8oz self-raising flour
1 Bramley apple (about 250g/9oz) peeled and chopped into pea-sized pieces

TO DECORATE
50g/2oz white chocolate
1 tbsp candied lemon peel, chopped
1 tbsp sugar 'coffee crystals'

Takes 2 hours • Serves 12

1 Preheat the oven to 160°C/fan 140°C/gas 3. Butter and line a 20cm/8in round cake tin. Put the dates in a bowl and cover with boiling water. Melt the butter in a pan, then stir in the sugar. Allow to cool slightly.
2 Drain the dates and chop them finely. Beat into the butter, eggs, ginger and lemon zest. Stir in the flour and apple. Spoon into the tin and put it on a baking sheet, then bake for 1¼ hours or until well risen. A skewer inserted into the cake should come out with a few moist crumbs sticking to it. Leave the cake to cool in the tin.
3 Break the chocolate into a heatproof bowl and melt over a pan of simmering water. Remove the cake from the tin. Trickle the chocolate over the cake, scatter with the candied lemon peel and coffee crystals and leave to set before serving.

• Per slice 376 kcalories, protein 4g, carbohydrate 57g, fat 16g, saturated fat 9g, fibre 2g, added sugar 30g, salt 0.53g

This fruity, crumbly loaf has loads of flavour but no added fat or sugar – ideal if you're watching your waistline.

Date, banana and rum loaf

250g pack stoned, ready-to-eat dates
2 small bananas or 1 large (140g/5oz total weight)
100g/4oz pecan halves (85g roughly chopped)
200g/8oz raisins
200g/8oz sultanas
100g/4oz fine polenta
2 tsp mixed spice
2 tsp baking powder
3 tbsp dark rum
2 egg whites
a few banana chips and 1 tsp sugar (optional), to decorate

Takes 1¼ hours • Serves 10

1 Preheat the oven to 180°C/fan 160°C/gas 4. Line a 900g/2lb loaf tin with non-stick baking paper, using a little oil to hold it in place. Put the dates into a small pan with 200ml/7fl oz boiling water and simmer for 5 minutes. Strain the date liquid into a jug and put the dates in a food processor. Add the banana and 100ml/3½fl oz of the date liquid to the dates and whiz until smooth. Mix the chopped nuts, dried fruit, polenta, spice and baking powder in a bowl, then add the date purée and the rum, and mix well.

2 Whisk the egg whites to soft peaks and fold into the cake mix. Tip into the tin (it will be quite full), then top with the remaining pecans and the banana chips and sugar, if using. Bake for 1 hour or until golden and crusty and a skewer comes out clean. Cool completely before cutting into slices.

• Per slice 310 kcalories, protein 5g, carbohydrate 57g, fat 8g, saturated fat 1g, fibre 3g, sugar 49g, salt 0.39g

This is so simple to make and is a delicious almondy twist on a traditional cherry cake. It's perfect to serve at Easter, as a change from simnel cake.

Cherry and almond cake

250g butter, softened, plus extra for greasing
175g/6oz golden caster sugar
5 eggs, beaten
250g/9oz self-raising flour, plus an extra 2 tbsp
1 tsp baking powder
zest of 1 orange, plus 2 tbsp of the juice
200g/8oz glacé cherries, halved
250g/9oz natural marzipan, coarsely grated (easiest if chilled beforehand)
½ tsp almond essence (optional)

TO DECORATE
100g/4oz icing sugar, sifted
50g/2oz flaked almonds, toasted
12 natural glacé cherries
zest of 1 orange

Takes 1 hour 50 minutes • Serves 12

1 Preheat the oven to 160°C/fan 140°C/ gas 3 and butter and line a 20cm/8in round, loose-bottomed tin. Whisk the butter and sugar until light and fluffy. Add the eggs, flour, baking powder, zest and juice, and whisk.
2 Toss the cherries in the extra two tablespoons of flour and fold into the batter along with the marzipan and almond essence (if using). Spoon into the tin and bake for 1½ hours, until risen and a skewer inserted comes out clean. Leave to cool in the tin for 10 minutes, then turn out on to a rack to cool.
3 Mix the icing sugar with one tablespoon of water to make a loose icing. Scatter the almonds over the top of the cake and position the twelve glacé cherries around the edge. Use a little icing to fix each in place. Drizzle over remaining icing. Finish with a little orange zest.

• Per slice 515 kcalories, protein 7g, carbohydrate 69g, fat 25g, saturated fat 12g, fibre 2g, added sugar 53g, salt 0.76g

This traditional fruit cake has been spiced up with lots of ginger for an intense, rich cake that's perfect for Christmas. You'd never know it's gluten and dairy-free either.

Gingered rich fruit cake

oil, for greasing
100g/4oz each dried currants, sultanas and raisins
225g/8oz each semi-dried figs and prunes, roughly chopped
200g tub crystallized ginger
100g/4oz stem ginger (from a jar), chopped
2 tbsp stem ginger syrup
4 tbsp Cointreau
1 tsp each ground ginger and mixed spice
zest of 2 lemons
150ml/5fl oz olive oil
175g/6oz light muscovado sugar
4 eggs
225g/8oz gluten-free flour
1 tsp gluten-free baking powder

FOR THE TOPPING
4 tbsp apricot jam
1 tbsp Cointreau
450g/1lb mixed fruit (including figs, prunes, dates and apricots)

Takes 2–3 hours, plus decorating
Serves 10–12

1 Preheat the oven to 140°C/fan 120°C/gas 1. Lightly oil a deep 25cm/10in round cake tin, and line it with a double layer of non-stick baking paper.
2 Mix together the dried fruits, gingers, syrup, Cointreau, spices and lemon zest, and set aside. In another bowl, whisk the olive oil, sugar and eggs until light and fluffy. Sift in the flour and baking powder, and tip in the fruit. Stir together well and spoon into the cake tin.
3 Bake for 2–2½ hours, or until a skewer inserted into the centre comes out clean. Check the cake towards the end of cooking and cover it if it begins to over-brown. Cool in the tin. Meanwhile, in a pan, melt the jam into the Cointreau, then cool. Remove the cake from the tin, arrange the fruit on the top and brush over the jam mixture.

• Per slice (for 10) 600 kcalories, protein 7g, carbohydrate 107g, fat 18g, saturated fat 3g, fibre 4g, added sugar 43g, salt 0.33g

The Swiss roll gets a makeover with this delicious lemony filling. If using shop-bought rather than homemade lemon curd in this recipe, add a little more fresh lemon juice for extra zest.

Lemon mascarpone roulade

6 eggs
175g/6oz golden caster sugar, plus extra for dusting
175g/6oz self-raising flour
1 heaped tsp caraway seeds (optional)
grated zest of 1 lemon
50g/2oz butter, melted

FOR THE FILLING
juice of 1 lemon
300g/10oz lemon curd
250g carton mascarpone
icing sugar, to dust

Takes 45 minutes • Serves 6

1 Preheat the oven to 200°C/fan 180°C/gas 6. Line a 27x40cm/11x16in Swiss roll tin with non-stick baking paper. Whisk the eggs and sugar together for 5 minutes, until light and fluffy. Fold in the flour, caraway seeds (if using) and lemon zest, then gradually fold in the butter. Tip the mix into the tin and bake for 12–15 minutes or until pale, but springy in the middle. Cool a little, then turn out on to a sheet of baking paper dusted with sugar, roll up and leave to cool.
2 While the sponge is cooling, mix the lemon juice and half the lemon curd with the mascarpone and set aside. When the sponge is completely cool, unroll it and spread with the mascarpone mix. Spread the remaining lemon curd over the top, then roll it up again. Dust with icing sugar to serve.

• Per slice 708 kcalories, protein 12g, carbohydrate 90g, fat 36g, saturated fat 18g, fibre 1g, sugar 57g, salt 0.8g

This updated quick-mix version of the Easter classic makes a perfect cut-and-come-again cake for the weekend.

Simple simnel cake

grated zest and juice of 1 orange
1 tbsp Cointreau
175g/6oz dried mixed fruit
50g/2oz whole glacé cherries
100g/4oz soft butter, diced
100g/4oz golden caster sugar
175g/6oz self-raising flour
2 eggs
1 tbsp milk
100g/4oz marzipan (rolled to the width and length of the tin)

FOR THE CARAMEL ALMONDS
100g/4oz caster sugar
50g/2oz whole blanched toasted almonds

FOR THE ICING
125g/4½oz icing sugar
zest of 1 orange
1–1½ tbsp fresh orange juice

Takes 1 hour 20 minutes • Serves 10

1 Preheat the oven to 160°C/fan 140°C/ gas 3. Mix the orange zest and juice, Cointreau, mixed fruit and cherries into a bowl. Grease and line a 900g/2lb loaf tin.
2 Put the butter, sugar, flour, eggs and milk in a bowl and beat until smooth. Stir in the fruit and their juices. Spoon half the mixture into the tin, then cover with the marzipan. Top with the rest of the cake mix and smooth the top. Bake for 1 hour or until risen and firm to the touch. Cool in the tin.
3 To make the caramel almonds, gently heat the sugar in a non-stick pan until it becomes a golden, liquid caramel. Add the almonds. Pour on to a greased baking sheet to set.
4 Mix together the icing ingredients, then pour it over the cake. Chop up the caramel, scatter it over the icing and allow to set.

• Per slice 425 kcalories, protein 5.4g, carbohydrate 72.5g, fat 14.3g, saturated fat 6g, fibre 1.6g, sugar 59.2g, salt 0.40g

The chewy toffees in this cake give it a delicious 'banoffee' flavour.

Banana and pecan fudge loaf

150g pack Werther's Original Chewy Toffees
2 ripe bananas, mashed (about 200g/8oz peeled weight)
2 medium eggs, beaten
100g/4oz butter, melted
100g/4oz toffee yogurt
100g/4oz light muscovado sugar
200g/8oz self-raising flour
½ tsp baking powder
100g/4oz pecan halves, roughly chopped

Takes 1–1½ hours • Serves 10–12

1 Preheat the oven to 160°C/fan 140°C/gas 3. Butter and line the base of a 900g/2lb loaf tin. Use wetted scissors to snip the toffees into small chunks,
2 Mix together the bananas, eggs, butter, toffee yogurt and sugar until well combined. Sift the flour and baking powder together and fold into the mixture, then fold in three quarters of the pecan nuts and half the chopped toffees.
3 Spoon the mixture into the tin and level the top. Sprinkle over the remaining nuts and toffees. Bake for 50–55 minutes or until the loaf has risen and feels springy. Cool in the tin, then remove and peel off the lining.

• Per slice (of 12) 300 kcalories, protein 4g, carbohydrate 35g, fat 17g, saturated fat 6.5g, fibre 1g, added sugar 15g, salt 0.5g

A classic Welsh tea bread that's packed with fruit and spices.

Sugar-crusted Bara Brith

400g/14oz luxury mixed fruit
75g pack dried cranberries
mug of hot, strong black tea
100g/4oz butter, plus extra for greasing
2 heaped tbsp orange marmalade
2 eggs, beaten
450g/1lb self-raising flour (try a mix of wholemeal and white)
175g/6oz light brown soft sugar
1 tsp each ground cinnamon and ground ginger
4 tbsp milk
50g/2oz crushed sugar cubes, to decorate

Takes 1¼–1½ hours, plus overnight soaking of fruit • Serves 12

1 Mix together the dried fruit and cranberries in a large bowl and pour over the hot tea. Cover and leave to soak overnight.
2 Preheat the oven to 180°C/fan 160°C/ gas 4. Butter and line the bottom of a 900g/2lb loaf tin. Melt the butter and marmalade together in a pan then cool for 5 minutes. Beat in the eggs. Drain any excess tea from the fruit. Mix the flour, sugar and spices together, stir in the fruit, butter mix and milk until combined. The batter should softly drop from the spoon, if not, add more milk.
3 Spoon into the tin and level the top. Sprinkle with the sugar and bake for 1–1¼ hours until dark golden and a skewer inserted comes out clean. Cover loosely with foil if it starts to over-colour before the middle is cooked. Cool in the tin before serving.

• Per slice 397 kcalories, protein 6g, carbohydrate 79g, fat 9g, saturated fat 5g, fibre 2g, sugar 50g, salt 0.58g

This deliciously moist cake is made extra-special with a tangy strawberry-flavoured icing.

Poppy seed and honey cake

140g/5oz self-raising flour, plus extra for dusting
100g/4oz golden caster sugar, plus extra for dusting
175g/6oz butter, softened
85g/3oz clear honey (try acacia for a delicate flavour)
3 medium eggs
25g/1oz cornflour
2 tbsp poppy seeds

FOR THE ICING
100g/4oz icing sugar
1½–2 tbsp sieved strawberry purée (made by crushing and sieving a handful of strawberries)

Takes 1 hour • Serves 8–10

1 Preheat the oven to 160°C/fan 140°C/gas 3. Butter a large ring tin (approx 20cm/8in), dust the buttered surface with one tablespoon each of flour and caster sugar, then tap out the excess.
2 Beat the butter, sugar and honey with electric beaters until pale and fluffy with a dropping consistency. Beat in the eggs one at a time. Mix the flour, cornflour and poppy seeds and fold into the creamed mixture.
3 Spoon the mixture into the tin, level the surface, then bake for about 35 minutes until risen and firm. Leave to cool slightly in the tin then carefully remove, easing the sides with a palette knife. Cool on a wire rack.
4 For the icing, mix both ingredients together and drizzle it over the cake while it's still on the rack. Leave to set. Transfer to a plate to serve.

• Per slice (for 10) 315 kcalories, protein 4g, carbohydrate 40g, fat 18g, saturated fat 10g, fibre 1g, added sugar 25g, salt 0.5g

Enjoy this indulgently dark coffee cake with a freshly brewed cup of coffee. Divine!

Coffee cake with pecan brittle

225g/8oz unsalted butter, softened
225g/8oz light muscovado sugar
4 eggs, beaten
225g/8oz self-raising flour
1 tsp baking powder
2 tbsp instant espresso coffee, mixed with 2 tbsp boiling water
85g/3oz pecan halves, finely chopped

FOR THE PECAN BRITTLE
100g/4oz granulated sugar
85g/3oz pecan

FOR THE COFFEE BUTTERCREAM
300g/10oz icing sugar
200g/8oz unsalted butter, softened
1 tbsp instant espresso coffee, mixed with 1 tbsp boiling water

Takes 1 hour 10 minutes • Serves 10

1 Preheat the oven to 180°C/ fan 160°C/ gas 4. Grease and line the base of two 20cm/8in sandwich tins. Place all of the cake ingredients into a mixer and beat until well blended. Divide between the tins then bake for 20–25 minutes or until a skewer comes out clean. Cool for 10 minutes in the tins then cool on a wire rack.

2 For the pecan brittle, heat the sugar and water gently in a pan until dissolved, then cook until golden. Stir in the pecans then tip out on to a greased baking sheet and leave to cool.

3 Beat the buttercream ingredients together until smooth then spread over the cakes. Sandwich one cake on top of the other. Shatter the pecan brittle and scatter it over the iced cake as decoration.

• Per slice 786 kcalories, protein 6.8g, carbohydrate 83g, fat 49.7g, saturated fat 23.8g, fibre 1.5g, sugar 65.5g, salt 0.48g

A stunning but simple idea for a birthday cake based on a basic sponge cake. Decorate with your choice of colourful lollipops and sweets.

Lollipop cake

280g/10oz butter, very well softened
280g/10oz golden caster sugar
6 medium eggs
200g/8oz self-raising flour
50g/2oz custard powder or cornflour
finely grated zest of 2 lemons
or oranges

TO DECORATE
about 6 tbsp thick lemon curd, plus
extra for brushing
½ × 454g pack ready-to-roll icing
lollipops
candles
jelly sweets or Smarties

Takes 1½ hours • Serves 12–16

1 Preheat the oven to 160°C/fan 140°C/gas 3. Butter and line the bottom of a 20cm/8in round cake tin. Beat together all the cake ingredients in a large bowl until creamy. Spoon the mixture into the tin, then bake for about 1 hour or until risen and springy to the touch. Leave to cool briefly in the tin, then turn the cake out and cool on a wire rack. If the cake peaks a bit, slice off the top to level it.
2 Cut the cake in half and sandwich back together with the lemon curd. Brush the top of the cake with a little more lemon curd. Roll out the icing and cut into a 20cm/8in round. Carefully place on top of the cake, smoothing it with your hands. Stick the lollipops into the icing at different levels, add the appropriate number of candles, then scatter on some jelly sweets or Smarties.

• Per slice (for 16) 353 kcalories, protein 4g, carbohydrate 49g, fat 17g, saturated fat 10g, fibre none, added sugar 42g, salt 0.7g

Everyone will love this tasty bake with its Bakewell-like filling and layer of tangy cherry jam.

Classic cherry and almond slice

375g pack ready-rolled shortcrust pastry
100g/4oz butter, softened
100g/4oz golden caster sugar
1 egg, beaten
25g/1oz ground rice
50g/2oz ground almonds
50g/2oz desiccated coconut
50g/2oz walnut halves, roughly chopped
5 tbsp cherry jam
100g/4oz glacé cherries

Takes 1 hour • Serves 16

1 Preheat the oven to 180°C/fan 160°C/ gas 4 and line the base of an 18x27cm/ 7x11in (or thereabouts) baking tin with greaseproof paper. Line the base and sides with the pastry, trim the edges, then chill while you make the filling.

2 Beat the butter and sugar together until fluffy, then gradually add the egg until creamy. Stir in the rice, almonds, coconut and nuts. Spread the jam over the pastry, then dollop the almond mix on top. (Don't worry if there are some little gaps, as the filling will spread during baking.)

3 Dot the cherries over the top of the cake mixture and bake for 40–45 minutes until light golden and set. Check after 30 minutes – if the top is browning too quickly, cover it loosely with greaseproof paper. Cool in the tin, then cut into slices.

• Per slice 275 kcalories, protein 3g, carbohydrate 27g, fat 18g, saturated fat 8g, fibre 1g, sugar 15g, salt 0.36g

A cross between a crumble and a plum pie, these slices make an irresistible addition to the tea table, or are a delicious dessert served warm with custard.

Plum and almond crumble slice

250g butter (this must be very cold)
225g/8oz caster sugar, plus extra for sprinkling
300g/10oz ground almonds
140g/5oz plain flour, plus 25g/1oz extra
2 eggs
1 tsp ground cinnamon, plus extra for sprinkling
1 tsp baking powder
approx. 6 plums, stoned and cut into sixths
50g/2oz flaked almonds

Takes about 1 hour • Serves 16

1 Preheat the oven to 180°C/fan 160°C/gas 4. Butter and line a 20x4x30cm/8x12in baking tin. Pulse the butter, sugar and ground almonds in a food processor until they resemble a rough crumble. Spoon half the mixture into a bowl. Set aside.
2 Add 140g/5oz of the flour into the mix and whiz until it just forms a dough. Tip this into the tin, press down well and bake for 15–20 minutes or until golden. Cool for 10 minutes.
3 To make the filling, tip all but a few tablespoons of the crumble mix back into the mixer. Add the eggs, extra flour, cinnamon and baking powder and whiz to a soft batter. Spread this over the cooled base.
4 Top the batter with the plums, a little extra sugar and cinnamon. Bake for 20 minutes. Sprinkle with the remaining crumble and the flaked almonds and cook for 20 minutes or until golden. Cool completely before slicing.

• Per slice 360 kcalories, protein 7g, carbohydrate 26g, fat 26g, saturated fat 9g, fibre 2g, sugar 18g, salt 0.37g

This sticky, crumbly bake is totally irresistible and makes a comforting pudding that comes straight from the tin.

Blueberry lemon cake with coconut crumble topping

300g/10oz butter, softened
425g/15oz caster sugar
zest of 1 lemon
6 eggs
250g/9oz self-raising flour
300g/10oz blueberries
200g/8oz desiccated coconut
200g/8oz lemon curd

Takes 1 hour • Serves 16

1 Preheat the oven to 180°C/fan 160°C/ gas 4 and grease and line a 20x30cm/8x12in cake tin. Beat 250g/9oz butter, 250g/9oz sugar, four of the eggs and all the zest until creamy. Fold in the flour and a third of the blueberries. Spoon the mixture into the tin. Sprinkle over another third of the blueberries. Bake for 20 minutes or until the surface is set.
2 For the topping, melt the rest of the butter, then stir in the coconut, remaining sugar and eggs until combined. Warm the lemon curd gently for a few minutes in a small pan until it is runny and pourable.
3 Scatter the remaining blueberries over the cake, drizzle with lemon curd then crumble over the coconut mixture. Bake for 20–25 minutes more or until the coconut is golden and the cake is cooked. Cool in the tin then cut into squares.

• Per square 446 kcalories, protein 5g, carbohydrate 50g, fat 27g, saturated fat 17g, fibre 43g, sugar 34g, salt 0.55g

If you like carrot cake you'll love this nifty tray bake, which is the ideal way to use up your leftover Hallowe'en pumpkin.

Hallowe'en pumpkin cake

300g/10oz self-raising flour
300g/10oz light muscovado sugar
3 tsp mixed spice
2 tsp bicarbonate of soda
175g/6oz sultanas
½ tsp salt
4 eggs, beaten
200g/8oz butter, melted
zest of 1 orange
1 tbsp fresh orange juice
500g/1lb 2oz pumpkin or butternut squash flesh (peeled weight), grated

FOR DRENCHING AND FROSTING
200g pack soft cheese
85g/3oz butter, softened
100g/4oz icing sugar, sifted
zest of 1 orange and juice of half

Takes 50 minutes • Serves 15, generously

1 Preheat the oven to 180°C/fan 160°C/ gas 4. Butter and line a 30x20cm/12x8in baking tin. Mix the first six ingredients in a bowl. Beat the eggs into the melted butter, stir in the zest, juice and pumpkin. Mix this with the dry ingredients. Pour the mixture into the tin. Bake for 30 minutes or until golden and springy. (Pumpkins vary in their water content so keep an eye on the cake towards the end of cooking – it may take less time.)
2 For the frosting, beat together the cheese, butter, icing sugar, orange zest and one teaspoon of the juice until smooth.
3 Cool the cake for 5 minutes then turn on to a wire rack. Prick with a skewer, drizzle with the remaining juice while warm, then cool completely. If you like, trim the edges. Beat the frosting and swirl it over the top of the cake.

• Per square (for 15) 408 kcalories, protein 5g, carbohydrate 52g, fat 21g, saturated fat 13g, fibre 1g, sugar 37g, salt 1.33g

A dark chocolate topping and melt-in-the-mouth almond shortbread gives this classic tray bake a grown-up twist.

Choc and nut caramel slice

175g/6oz plain flour
25g/1oz cornflour
50g/2oz golden caster sugar
85g/3oz whole blanched almonds,
toasted then finely chopped
pinch of salt
140g/5oz unsalted butter, cold and
cut into cubes
seeds from 1 vanilla pod

FOR THE CARAMEL
225g/8½oz golden caster sugar
142ml carton single cream
50g/2oz butter, cubed
½ tsp salt

FOR THE TOPPING
200g bar plain chocolate (70%
cocoa solids)
85g/3oz butter

Takes 1 hour 20 minutes, plus chilling
Serves 16

1 Preheat the oven to 160°C/fan 140°C/gas 3 and lightly butter a 20x23cm/8x9in shallow baking tin. Sift the flours together, stir in the sugar, almonds and a pinch of salt. Rub in the butter and vanilla seeds to make fine crumbs. Press the mix into the tin using the back of a spoon. Put the tin in the freezer for 5 minutes. Bake for 35–40 minutes. Cool.
2 For the caramel, put the sugar and 100ml/3½fl oz water in a heavy-based pan, heat gently until the sugar dissolves, then turn up the heat until it turns a very dark amber. Stir in the cream in four additions until smooth – take care as it will bubble up. Stir in the butter and salt. Pour over the shortbread and cool.
3 For the topping, melt the chocolate and butter together, then pour over the caramel and smooth with the back of a spoon. Chill until firm, at least 30 minutes, before cutting.

• Per slice 358 kcalories, protein 4g, carbohydrate 34g, fat 24g, saturated fat 13g, fibre 2g, sugar 22g, salt 0.15g

You can't beat American-style cookies packed with big chunks of chocolate and nuts – the perfect sophisticated biscuit.

Chocolate-chunk pecan cookies

200g/8oz plain chocolate (70% cocoa solids), broken into squares
100g/4oz butter, chopped
50g/2oz light muscovado sugar
85g/3oz golden caster sugar
1 tsp vanilla extract
1 egg, beaten
100g/4oz whole pecan nuts
100g/4oz plain flour
1 tsp bicarbonate of soda

Takes 25 minutes • Makes 12

1 Preheat the oven to 180°C/fan 160°C/gas 4. Melt 85g/3oz of the chocolate in the microwave on High for 1 minute, or over a pan of simmering water. Beat in the butter, sugars, vanilla and egg until smooth, then stir in three-quarters of both the nuts and remaining chocolate, then the flour and bicarbonate of soda.

2 Heap twelve spoonfuls of the mixture, spaced apart, on two baking sheets (don't spread it), then poke in the reserved nuts and chocolate. Bake for 12 minutes until firm, then leave to cool on the sheets. The cookies can be stored in a tin for up to 3 days.

• Per cookie 294 kcalories, protein 4g, carbohydrate 27g, fat 20g, saturated fat 8g, fibre 2g, sugar 17g, salt 0.44g

Make these with the kids for an hour of messy fun – and get some deliciously crumbly cookies to show for it.

Ginger choc chip cookies

85g/3oz light muscovado sugar
200g/8oz butter, softened, plus extra for greasing
250g/9oz self-raising flour
2 tbsp golden syrup
1 tsp vanilla extract
100g/4oz plain chocolate drops or plain chocolate, chopped
50g/2oz preserved ginger from a jar, or crystallized ginger, roughly chopped

Takes 20 minutes, plus chilling
Makes 20 cookies

1 Butter and line two large baking sheets with non-stick baking paper. Preheat the oven to 200°C/fan 180°C/gas 6. Beat together the sugar and butter until pale and creamy. Stir in the remaining ingredients until you have a soft dough. Roll the dough into walnut-sized pieces and space them out generously on the lined baking sheets. If you have time, leave the dough to chill in the fridge for 30 minutes at this point.

2 Bake the cookies for 12–15 minutes until lightly golden; they will still feel quite soft in the middle. Leave on baking sheets until firm, about 5 minutes, then transfer to a wire rack to cool completely.

• Per cookie 169 kcalories, protein 1g, carbohydrate 20g, fat 10g, saturated fat 6g, fibre 1g, added sugar 11g, salt 0.28g

These luscious bites are great for coffee lovers, and the all-in-one pan method means they're simple to make.

Moccachino slices

100g/4oz butter
225g/8½oz dark brown soft sugar
2 eggs
3 tbsp espresso coffee (or mix
3 tbsp boiling water with 1 tbsp
instant coffee)
2 tsp baking powder
125g/4½oz plain flour

FOR THE TOPPING
284ml carton soured cream
280g/10oz white chocolate, broken
into chunks
4 tsp caster sugar
cocoa powder, to dust

Takes 45 minutes • Makes 12

1 Preheat the oven to 180°C/fan 160°C/gas 4 and butter and line the base and sides of a baking tin approx 30x23cm/12x9in with non-stick baking paper. Melt the butter in a large pan, stir in the sugar and mix well. Take off the heat and stir in the eggs and coffee. Tip in the baking powder and flour, then mix well. Pour into the tin and bake for 20 minutes. Cool, then turn out on to a board.
2 Meanwhile, melt together the soured cream, white chocolate and sugar in a small bowl set over a pan of simmering water. Stir well, then leave to cool for 15 minutes. Spread this mixture all over the top of the cake. Shake over the cocoa powder to dust lightly, then leave to set. Cut into 12 squares and serve.

• Per slice 372 kcalories, protein 5g, carbohydrate 45g, fat 20g, saturated fat 12g, fibre 1g, sugar 36g, salt 0.51g

Made with olive oil spread and plenty of oats to help keep down cholesterol levels, these oat cookies are a fantastic healthy treat for snacking adults and children alike.

Healthier oat cookies

100g/4oz olive oil spread
50g/2oz light muscovado sugar
2 tbsp clear honey
¼ tsp ground mixed spice
100g/4oz self-raising flour
100g/4oz porridge oats
50g/2oz raisins

Takes 30 minutes • Makes 15

1 Preheat the oven to 170°C/fan 150°C/ gas 3½. Put the spread, sugar and honey into a heatproof bowl, then microwave on High for 1 minute until everything's just melted (or melt it all together in a small pan). Stir in the mixed spice, flour, oats and raisins, then mix together to combine.

2 Line two baking sheets with non-stick baking paper and spoon tablespoons of the mixture, spaced well apart, on to the prepared sheets. Flatten the tops slightly with a fork. Bake for 15 minutes or until golden brown and crisp on the base. Leave to cool, then store in an airtight container.

• Per cookie 135 kcalories, protein 2g, carbohydrate 17g, fat 7g, saturated fat 1g, fibre 1g, sugar 7g, salt 0.07g

A little like spicy, fruited flapjacks, these wholesome cookies will be a welcome addition to any lunchbox or biscuit tin.

Bumper oat cookies

175g/6oz butter
175g/6oz demerara sugar
100g/4oz golden syrup
85g/3oz plain flour
½ tsp bicarbonate of soda
250g/9oz porridge oats
1 tsp ground cinnamon
100g/4oz ready-to-eat dried apricots, chopped
80g pack dried sour cherries
100g/4oz preserved stem ginger, chopped
2 tbsp boiling water
1 medium egg, beaten

Takes 45–50 minutes • Makes 18

1 Preheat the oven to 180°C/fan 160°C/gas 4. Line several baking sheets with non-stick baking paper. Warm the butter, sugar and golden syrup in a large pan until the butter has melted. Stir in the flour, bicarbonate of soda, oats, cinnamon, dried fruits and ginger, then the water and egg. Leave to cool until easy to handle.

2 With dampened hands, shape the mixture into 18 large balls, then flatten them on to the baking sheets – allowing plenty of space for them to spread. Bake for 15–20 minutes or until golden for a soft, chewy cookie. For a crisper one, reduce the heat to 160°C/fan 140°C/gas 3 and bake for 5–10 minutes more. Leave the cookies on the sheets for a few minutes, then lift on to to a cooling wire rack to cool completely.

• Per cookie 236 kcalories, protein 3g, carbohydrate 37g, fat 10g, saturated fat 5g, fibre 2g, added sugar 13g, salt 0.3g

Bursting with berries, this is the perfect summer tray bake for afternoon tea in the garden or a picnic.

Raspberry and almond tray bake

250g/9oz self-raising flour
50g/2oz ground almonds
200g/8oz butter, diced
280g/10oz golden granulated sugar
50g/2oz desiccated coconut
2 medium eggs
350–450g/12oz–1lb fresh raspberries
(or 340g pack frozen)

Takes 1¼–1½ hours, plus any defrosting • Serves 16–24

1 Preheat the oven to 180°C/fan 160°C/gas 4. Butter an oblong cake tin (about 30x17cm/12x7in). Tip the flour, ground almonds, butter and sugar into a food processor and whiz just until the butter is evenly distributed – or rub together by hand. Remove 85g/3oz of the mix, stir in the coconut and set side. Add the eggs to the remaining mixture in the food processor and whiz quickly – or mix with a wooden spoon. It doesn't need to be smooth.
2 Spread this mixture over the base of the tin, then scatter over half the raspberries. Sprinkle with the coconut mixture and bake for 45 minutes. Dot the remaining fruit over the surface and cook for a further 15 minutes or until firm to the touch. Cool in the tin and cut into slices, squares, or whatever shape you want.

• Per slice (for 24) 179 kcalories, protein 3g, carbohydrate 21g, fat 10g, saturated fat 6g, fibre 1g, added sugar 12g, salt 0.3g

This simple-to-whip-up apple cake can be cut into bars or squares and is best served warm with clotted cream or a good vanilla ice cream. Delicious!

Dorset apple tray bake

450g/1lb Bramley apples
juice of ½ lemon
225g/8½oz butter, softened
280g/10oz golden caster sugar
4 eggs
2 tsp vanilla extract
350g/12oz self-raising flour
2 tsp baking powder
demerara sugar, to sprinkle

Takes 1 hour 10 minutes • Serves 16

1 Preheat the oven to 180°C/fan 160°C/ gas 4. Butter and line a rectangular baking tin (approx. 27x20cm/11x8in). Peel, core and thinly slice the apples then squeeze over the lemon juice. Set to one side.
2 Place the butter, caster sugar, eggs, vanilla, flour and baking powder into a large bowl and mix well until smooth. Spread half the mixture into the prepared tin. Arrange half the apples over the top of the mixture, then repeat the layers. Sprinkle over the demerara sugar.
3 Bake for 45–50 minutes or until golden and springy to the touch. Leave to cool for 10 minutes, then turn out of the tin and remove the paper. Cut into bars or squares.

• Per square 285 kcalories, protein 4g, carbohydrate 39g, fat 13g, saturated fat 8g, fibre 1g, sugar 23g, salt 0.66g

These are a twist on classic iced party rings, but the dough and icing would work just as well to make biscuits in other shapes, such as stars or hearts.

Birthday biscuits

250g/9oz plain white flour
85g/3oz golden caster sugar
175g/6oz unsalted butter (at room temperature), cubed
2 tbsp lemon curd
250g/9oz white icing sugar, sifted
1 tbsp strawberry fruit spread (we used St Dalfour)

Takes 40 minutes • Makes 24

1 Preheat the oven to 180°C/ fan 160°C/ gas 4. Whiz the flour, sugar and butter in a food processor to make crumbs. Pulse a little more to form a ball. Turn the dough out on to a sheet of lightly floured non-stick baking paper. Roll out to the thickness of two £1 coins. Stamp out 24 rounds using a 5cm/2in fluted cutter and cut out the centres with the end of a piping nozzle. Lift the rounds on to baking sheets. Bake for 10 minutes until pale golden. Cool on a wire rack.
2 Mix the lemon curd with two tablespoons of boiling water until smooth. Sieve in 175g/6oz of the icing sugar, stir until smooth. Mix the jam with two teaspoons of boiling water, sieve in the remaining icing sugar.
3 Spoon lemon icing over the biscuits, then drizzle over the pink icing. Set for 20 minutes.

• Per biscuit 149 kcalories, protein 1g, carbohydrate 24g, fat 6g, saturated fat 4g, fibre none, sugar 16g, salt 0.01g

Try making these for the kids instead of icecream cones, or for a delicious, smarter dessert replace the cookies with indulgent Belgian chocolate-dipped biscuits.

Cookie ice-cream sandwiches

500ml carton vanilla or chocolate
ice cream
150g pack chocolate chip cookies
100g/4oz blueberries or raspberries

Takes 15 minutes • Makes 10

1 Take the ice cream out of the freezer 10 minutes before you want to make the sandwiches. Lay half the biscuits out on a baking sheet lined with non-stick baking paper.

2 Mix the berries roughly into the ice cream, then scoop a little of the mixture on to each biscuit on the tray. Top with the remaining biscuits to make a sandwich, squish it down a little and eat straight away, or return them to the freezer until needed.

• Per sandwich 127 kcalories, protein 2g, carbohydrate 16.4g, fat 6.4g, saturated fat 2g, fibre 0.5g, sugar 11g, salt 0.18g

Making your own cereal bars is easy and really satisfying –
particularly as you know exactly what's in them.

Squidgy muesli bars

175g/6oz light muscovado sugar
100g/4oz olive oil spread
50g/2oz clear honey
300g/10oz high-fibre muesli
50g/2oz dried mixed fruit, chopped
1 tbsp golden linseed or sesame
seeds

Takes 30 minutes • Makes 12

1 Preheat the oven to 180°C/fan 160°C/
gas 4. Grease and line an 18cm/7in square
tin with non-stick baking paper.
2 Put the sugar, olive oil spread and honey in
a pan and heat until the spread has melted.
Stir well then mix in the high-fibre muesli and
the mixed fruit. Spoon into the prepared tin
and flatten the top with the back of a spoon.
Sprinkle over the linseed or sesame seeds
and bake for 20 minutes or until golden
brown. Leave to cool in the tin for at least
30 minutes, then cut into 12 bars.

• Per bar 237 kcalories, protein 3g, carbohydrate 36g,
fat 10g, saturated fat 2g, fibre 2g, sugar 23g,
salt 0.05g

Kids will just love these jammy biscuits – and they're simple enough that they can get involved in making them.

Smiley raspberry cookies

250g/9oz butter, softened
140g/5oz caster sugar
1 egg yolk
2 tsp vanilla extract
300g/10oz plain flour
1 tsp ground cinnamon

FOR THE FILLING
6 tbsp raspberry jam
6 tbsp icing sugar

TO DECORATE
50g/2oz icing sugar, sifted

Takes 35 minutes, plus chilling and decorating • Makes 14

1 Beat the butter and sugar in a large bowl, then add the egg yolk and vanilla. Beat briefly to combine. Sift in the flour and cinnamon and stir well – use your hands to give it a good mix. Shape into two balls, wrap, then chill for 20–30 minutes.
2 Preheat the oven to 180°C/fan 160°C/gas 4. Roll out the dough balls on a floured surface, then stamp out 14 biscuits from each using a 8cm/3in cutter. Transfer the biscuit shapes to lined baking sheets. Using a 5cm/2in cutter, cut out the 'noses' from half the biscuits. Bake for 10–12 minutes until pale golden, then cool on a wire rack.
3 Mix the jam and icing sugar, and spoon a little on to each whole biscuit. Carefully sandwich the other biscuits on top. To decorate, mix a few drops of water with the icing sugar, then use to pipe on faces.

• Per biscuit 295 kcalories, protein 2g, carbohydrate 39g, fat 15g, saturated fat 10g, fibre 1g, sugar 22g, salt 0.29g

These tempting cookies make pretty, festive Christmas-tree decorations. Make sure you pierce a hole in the top before baking, though, so you can easily thread a ribbon through once cool.

Spiced Christmas tree cookies

85g/3oz butter, softened, plus extra
for greasing
100g/4oz caster sugar
1 egg, beaten
1 tsp vanilla extract
2 tsp mixed spice
2 tbsp golden syrup
250g/9oz plain flour
½ tsp baking powder
icing sugar or granulated sugar,
to decorate

Takes 20 minutes, plus chilling
Makes 24

1 Beat the butter and sugar until pale, then add the egg slowly, beating as you go. Stir in the vanilla, spice, golden syrup, flour and baking powder. If it is very sticky, add a little more flour. Shape into a flat disc then wrap and chill for 1 hour.

2 Preheat the oven to 180°C/ fan 160°C/ gas 4 and grease a couple of baking sheets. Roll out half of the dough until it is the thickness of two £1 coins, then cut out twelve trees using a 7.5cm/3in cutter. Repeat with the remaining dough. Lift the cookies on to the baking sheets then bake for 10 minutes until just golden around the edges.

3 To decorate, either scatter them with granulated sugar before baking or dust with icing sugar when cooked.

• Per cookie 86 kcalories, protein 1.3g, carbohydrate 13.7g, fat 3.2g, saturated fat 1.9g, fibre 0.3g, sugar 5.9g, salt 0.10g

Lemon drizzle cake is a teatime classic – adding blueberries and cooking it in a ring mould gives it that extra-special finish.

Lemon blueberry cake

175g/6oz butter, softened, plus extra for greasing
300g/10oz sugar
4 eggs, lightly beaten
zest of 1 lemon
142ml carton soured cream
250g/9oz plain flour
2 tsp baking powder
pinch of salt
150g punnet blueberries

FOR THE ICING
100g/4oz icing sugar
4 tbsp fresh lemon juice

Takes about 1 hour • Serves 8

1 Preheat the oven to 180°C/fan 160°C/gas 4. Beat the butter and sugar until soft and creamy. Beat in the eggs a little at a time, then add the lemon zest. Fold in the soured cream then the flour, baking powder and a pinch of salt. Carefully mix the blueberries into the batter.
2 Butter a deep, 23cm/9in diameter ring tin (if ridged, it may be easier to use an oil spray to get in the corners). Spoon in the mixture then level the top. Bake for 45–55 minutes or until springy and a skewer inserted into the middle comes out clean. Leave to cool for 10 minutes. Turn out of the tin on to a wire rack set over a large plate or tray. Cool.
3 For the icing, mix together the icing sugar and lemon juice, drizzle it over the cake with a spoon and allow to set.

• Per slice 608 kcalories, protein 7g, carbohydrate 79g, fat 31g, saturated fat 18g, fibre 2g, sugar 55g, salt 0.84g

This light, creamy raspberry cake makes a sublimely sweet summer treat.

Raspberry layer cake

200g/8oz caster sugar
200g/8oz butter, softened
4 eggs, beaten
200g/8oz self-raising flour
1 tsp baking powder
icing sugar, to decorate

FOR THE SYRUP
85g/3oz caster sugar
50ml/2fl oz almond liqueur

FOR THE FILLING
284ml carton double cream
250g carton mascarpone
3 tbsp caster sugar
150g punnet raspberries

Takes 50 minutes, plus overnight chilling • Serves 8

1 Preheat the oven to 190°C/fan 170°C/gas 5. Butter and line two 20cm/8in sandwich tins. In a bowl, beat together all the cake ingredients until smooth. Spoon equally into the tins, then bake for 25–30 minutes, until golden and springy when gently pressed. Turn the cakes out on to a wire rack.
2 For the syrup, heat the sugar, two tablespoons of water and the liqueur together until the sugar has dissolved. Cool a little. Use a large serrated knife to cut each cake in half. Brush the syrup all over the four pieces of cake.
3 For the filling, whip the cream until it forms soft peaks. Beat the mascarpone and sugar in a large bowl to loosen. Fold into the cream. Layer the fruit, cream and sponges, starting and finishing with a layer of sponge. Press down lightly on the finished layer cake, wrap it tightly in cling film and chill overnight.

• Per slice 819 kcalories, protein 8g, carbohydrate 68g, fat 58g, saturated fat 33g, fibre 2g, sugar 50g, salt 1.02g

This patisserie-style cake is simpler to make than you'd think. A little saffron adds a gorgeous golden hue to the sponge.

Upside-down sticky apricot cake

85g/3oz golden caster sugar
6 apricots, halved

FOR THE BATTER
200g/8oz butter
175g/6oz golden caster sugar
2 eggs
75ml/2½fl oz full-fat milk
pinch of saffron strands diluted in a little warm water (optional)
140g/5oz plain flour
140g/5oz self-raising flour
100g/4oz ground almonds

Takes 1 hour • Serves 12

1 Tip the sugar into a deep, ovenproof frying pan. Place over a high heat until caramelized, remove from the heat, then lay the apricots, cut side down, in the caramel, quartering some of them to fit into the gaps. Set aside. Preheat the oven to 180°C/fan 160°C/gas 4.
2 Using an electric whisk, cream the butter and sugar together. Beat in the eggs one at a time, then the milk and saffron, if using. Fold in the flours and ground almonds, then beat until combined.
3 Spoon dollops of the batter over the apricots and smooth over with the back of a spoon. Bake for 40 minutes or until risen and golden. Remove from the oven and leave to sit for 10 minutes. Invert the cake on to a plate and leave to cool. Serve with crème fraîche, if you like.

• Per slice 552 kcalories, protein 9g, carbohydrate 66g, fat 30g, saturated fat 14g, fibre 3g, sugar 39g, salt 0.62g

A homely bake that's perfect served with tea or as a truly comforting dessert.

Spiced apple cake

140g/5oz butter, softened
200g/8oz caster sugar
2 eggs, beaten
200g/8oz self-raising flour
½ tsp ground cloves
¼ tsp grated fresh nutmeg
450g/1lb Bramley apples, peeled, cored and thickly sliced
icing sugar, to dust

Takes 2 hours • Serves 12

1 Preheat the oven to 180°C/fan 160°C/ gas 4, then butter and line a deep 20cm/8in round cake tin. Put the butter and sugar into a large bowl and beat together until pale and creamy. Add the eggs, a little at a time, until light and fluffy. Mix the flour with the cloves and nutmeg, then fold into the eggy mixture.
2 Spread half the mix over the bottom of the tin, then cover with the apple slices. Dot the rest of the mix over the apples, then bake for 1½hours or until a skewer comes out clean. (It will get quite dark on the top before it's done in the middle.) Leave the cake in the tin to cool – it might sink a bit – then dust with icing sugar before serving with crème fraîche or thick cream.

• Per slice 238 kcalories, protein 3g,carbohydrate 34g, fat 11g, saturated fat 6g, fibre 1g, sugar 22g, salt 0.37g

Peaches and raspberries are really good partners and especially good baked into this soft vanilla cake topped with cinnamon crumble.

Peach and raspberry buckle

175g/6oz self-raising flour
200g/8oz butter, softened
2 tbsp demerara sugar
2 tsp ground cinnamon
175g/6oz caster sugar
3 eggs
2 tsp vanilla extract
3 peaches, stoned and sliced
200g/8oz raspberries, fresh or frozen

Takes 1 hour 5 minutes, plus any defrosting • Serves 8

1 Preheat the oven to 180°C/fan 160°C/gas 4. Butter and line the base of a 23cm/9in square tin. For the crumble mix, put two tablespoons of flour and 25g/1oz of the butter in a bowl along with the demerara sugar and cinnamon. Rub the ingredients between your fingers until it resembles breadcrumbs.
2 Tip the remaining flour and butter and the caster sugar, eggs and vanilla in a bowl, then beat until well combined. Lightly fold in half the peaches and raspberries, then spread the mixture over the prepared tin.
3 Scatter over the remaining fruit, then sprinkle with the crumble mix. Bake for 45–50 minutes or until light golden, then cool for 10 minutes and remove from the tin. Cut into squares and serve warm with cream or ice cream for dessert, or cold for tea.

• Per square 437 kcalories, protein 6g, carbohydrate 53g, fat 24g, saturated fat 14g, fibre 2g, sugar 33g, salt 0.72g

Crisp choux pastry, fruit, cream and a wicked caramel sauce – the
perfect decadent dinner-party dessert for a warm summer evening.

Fruity choux buns with caramel sauce

85g/3oz butter
100g/4oz plain flour, sifted
pinch of salt
3 eggs, beaten

FOR THE CARAMEL SAUCE
50g/2oz butter
5 tbsp light muscavado sugar
142ml carton double cream

FOR THE FILLING
142 or 284ml carton double cream
(depending on how creamy you
like your choux buns)
1 tbsp icing sugar, sifted
3 tbsp dessert wine (sweet Muscat
works well)
2 ripe peaches, stoned and sliced
150g pack blueberries

Takes 40 minutes, plus cooling
Serves 6

1 Put the butter and 200ml/7fl oz cold water
into a pan and bring to a rolling boil. Take off
the heat and quickly tip in the flour and salt.
Whisk the mixture to a smooth paste that
leaves the sides of the pan. Cool on a plate.
2 Preheat the oven to 200°C/fan 180°C/
gas 6 and line a baking sheet. Return the
paste to the pan and beat in the eggs, little
by little; stop when you have a shiny paste
that drops easily from a spoon.
3 Spoon on to the sheet in six round blobs.
Bake for 20–25 minutes or until dark golden.
Make a hole in the base of each bun to let
out the steam. Bake for 5 more minutes. Cool
on a wire rack then cut each bun in half.
4 For the sauce, heat everything together for
5 minutes, stirring, until silky. Whip the cream,
sugar and wine together. Spoon the cream
and fruit into the buns. Drizzle over the sauce.

• Per bun (using 142ml cream) 589 kcalories,
protein 7g, carbohydrate 34g, fat 48g, saturated fat
27g, fibre 2g, sugar 21g, salt 0.75g

A beautifully moist, gluten-free cake that's packed with zingy citrus flavours and makes a wonderful alternative to the traditional Christmas cake.

Fruit-filled clementine cake

4 clementines
200g/8oz unsalted butter, softened,
plus extra for greasing
200g/8oz dark brown soft sugar
3 eggs, beaten
1 teaspoon ground cinnamon
1 tsp mixed spice
pinch of ground cloves
100g/4oz ground almonds
140g/5oz polenta
1 tsp baking powder (gluten-free,
if you prefer)
140g/5oz raisins
140g/5oz sultanas
140g/5oz currants
100g/4oz glacé cherries, quartered
2 tbsp brandy

FOR THE TOPPING
140g/5oz caster sugar
4 clementines, cut into 5mm slices
icing sugar, to decorate (most are gluten-free, but check the packaging)

Takes 2½–3 hours • Serves 8–10

1 For the cake, place the clementines in a pan, cover with water and simmer for 1 hour or until tender. Drain, cool, then finely chop.
2 Preheat the oven to 180°C/fan 160°C/gas 4. Butter and line a 20cm/8in cake tin. Cream the butter and sugar until pale, then add the eggs, spices, ground almonds, polenta and baking powder. Beat together. Fold in the dried fruit, clementines and brandy. Spoon into the tin then bake for 1 hour 10 minutes. Turn down to 160°C/fan 140°C/gas 3 after 30 minutes. Loosely cover with non-stick baking paper for the final 20 minutes to prevent over-browning. Cool.
3 For the topping, heat the sugar in 140ml/5fl oz water until dissolved. Simmer the clementines in the syrup (keep the slices submerged with a circle of greaseproof paper) for 45 minutes or until translucent. Dust the cake with icing sugar. Arrange the clementine slices, overlapping, on top.

• Per slice 695 kcalories, protein 9g, carbohydrate 93g, fat 34g, saturated fat 15g, fibre 3g, sugar 83g, salt 0.36g

This irresistible cake has the lightness of a sponge but the richness of a cheesecake. The cake base can also be used for other fruit, such as peaches, nectarines or apricots.

Plum, almond and ricotta cake

250g carton ricotta
140g/5oz butter, melted
4 eggs, beaten
225g/8oz golden caster sugar, plus 1 tbsp for the top
250g/9oz self-raising flour
200g pack ground almonds
4 tbsp plum or apricot jam
5 plums, quartered (we used yellow plums)
handful of flaked almonds, toasted
icing sugar, to dust

Takes 1 hour 50 minutes • Serves 10

1 Preheat the oven to 180°C/fan 160°C/gas 4. In a bowl, beat the ricotta, butter, eggs and sugar together, then fold in the flour and ground almonds. Spoon half the batter into a greased and lined 23cm/9in round cake tin. Evenly blob the jam over the middle, then cover with the remaining batter.

2 Arrange the plum quarters over the top. Sprinkle over remaining sugar, then bake for 1½hours until risen and golden and the plums have shrivelled and caramelized. Leave the cake to cool slightly, then remove from the tin and leave to cool on a wire rack. Scatter with the flaked almonds, dust with icing sugar and serve cut in slices.

• Per slice 518 kcalories, protein 12.5g, carbohydrate 53.8g, fat 29.5g, saturated fat 10.7g, fibre 2.8g, sugar 34.6g, salt 0.61g

This is a kind of right-way-up upside-down cake, but however you look at it, it makes a perfect teatime treat.

Apple and blackberry traycake

175g/6oz butter, plus extra for greasing
300g/10oz plain flour, plus extra for dusting
4 Bramley apples (approx. 800g/ 1lb 12oz)
squeeze of fresh lemon juice
284ml carton whipping cream
225g/8oz golden caster sugar, plus 1 tbsp for sprinkling
3 eggs
300g/10oz blackberries

Takes about 1 hour 15 minutes
Serves 8

1 Preheat the oven to 200°C/fan 180°C/ gas 6. Grease a small roasting tin (about 30x20cm/12x8in) with butter, dust with a little flour, then set aside. Peel, core and slice the apples into rings, then toss in a little lemon juice to stop them going brown.
2 Tip the cream and butter into a pan, bring to the boil, then set aside. Whisk the sugar with the eggs until they thicken and turn pale, about 3 minutes. Whisk the buttery cream into the eggs, then fold in the flour until completely smooth.
3 Pour the batter into the tin and arrange the apple slices over the top. Scatter over the blackberries, then sprinkle with the remaining sugar. Bake for 50 minutes–1 hour or until golden and beginning to pull away from the sides of the tin. Leave to cool in the tin and serve cut into squares.

• Per square 587 kcalories, protein 7g, carbohydrate 64g, fat 35g, saturated fat 21g, fibre 3g, sugar 42g, salt 1.01g

This wonderfully moist cake is reminiscent of an old-fashioned gingerbread – dense and full of spice.

Rhubarb spice cake

140g/5oz butter, softened, plus extra for greasing
300g/10oz self-raising flour
2 tsp mixed spice
1 tsp ground ginger
100g/4oz dark muscovado sugar
250g/9oz golden syrup
1 tsp bicarbonate of soda
2 eggs, beaten
300g/10oz rhubarb, cut into short lengths
icing sugar, for dusting

Takes 1 hour 10 minutes • Serves 12

1 Preheat the oven to 180°C/fan 160°C/ gas 4 and put the kettle on. Butter and line a deep 20cm/8in square cake tin. Sift the flour and spices into a bowl. In a food processor, beat together the butter and sugar until light and fluffy, then beat in the golden syrup. Dissolve the bicarbonate of soda in 200ml/ 7fl oz boiling water, then gradually pour it through the spout of the processor. Pulse in the flour, then add the eggs, mixing briefly. Remove the bowl from the processor and gently stir in the rhubarb.
2 Pour the mixture into the tin and bake for 50–60 minutes or until the cake feels firm to the touch and springs back when pressed. Cool in the tin for 5 minutes, then turn out and cool on a wire rack. Dust with icing sugar.

• Per slice 290 kcalories, protein 4g, carbohydrate 46g, fat 11g, saturated fat 7g, fibre 1g, sugar 27g, salt 0.89g

This scrumptious cake gives a serious nod to nostalgia – but tastes far better than you'll remember.

Pineapple and almond upside-down cake

85g/3oz butter
85g/3oz dark muscovado sugar
85g/3oz flaked toasted almonds
1 pineapple, peeled, cored and sliced, any juices reserved
100g/4oz natural glacé cherries

FOR THE BATTER
250g/9oz butter, softened
250g/9oz light muscovado sugar
4 eggs
200g/8oz plain flour
2 tsp baking powder
50g/2oz ground almonds
2 tbsp pineapple juice or rum

Takes 1 hour • Serves 8

1 Preheat the oven to 190°C/fan 170°C/gas 5. Cream the butter and sugar, and liberally brush over the bottom and sides of a 23cm/9in square tin. Scatter over the toasted almonds so that some stick to the sides and line the base with overlapping pineapple slices. Decorate with the cherries.

2 Tip all of the batter ingredients into a food processor and blitz until smooth. Pour the batter over the pineapple and bake for 50 minutes–1 hour until puffed up and golden. Leave the cake to relax for just a few minutes, then turn out, cut into squares and eat straight away with lashings of custard.

• Per square 781 kcalories, protein 11g, carbohydrate 82g, fat 48g, saturated fat 24g, fibre 3g, sugar 62g, salt 1.17g

Give sponge an Italian twist with this easy-to-make polenta cake, studded with intense bursts of raspberry.

Raspberry and lemon polenta cake

225g/8oz very soft butter
225g/8oz caster sugar, plus 1 tbsp for dusting
½ tsp vanilla extract
zest of 1½ lemons
4 eggs, beaten
175g/6oz fine polenta
50g/2oz plain flour
1½ tsp baking powder
200g/8oz frozen raspberries, left frozen
icing sugar, for dusting

FOR THE FILLING
100g/4oz soft cheese (at room temperature)
1 tbsp icing sugar or more, to taste
zest of ½ lemon, plus a squeeze of juice
142ml carton double cream
100g/4oz frozen raspberries, defrosted

Takes 50 minutes, plus defrosting
Serves 8

1 Preheat the oven to 190°C/fan 170°C/gas 5. Butter and line two 20cm/8in sandwich tins. Beat the butter, caster sugar, vanilla and zest together until creamy. Gradually beat in the eggs until pale and fluffy. Mix the dry ingredients, then fold into the batter.

2 Spoon half the batter into each tin and level the top. Scatter over the raspberries and poke them in gently. Sprinkle one of the sponges with the extra tablespoon of sugar. Bake for 30 minutes or until risen and golden. Cool in the tin for 10 minutes, then on a wire rack.

3 Beat the soft cheese with the icing sugar, zest and a little juice to loosen, if it needs it. Lightly whip the cream then fold into the cheese. Fold in the defrosted raspberries. Use the filling to sandwich the sponges together, placing the sugar-crusted one on top, and serve dusted with more icing sugar.

• Per slice 608 kcalories, protein 8g, carbohydrate 58g, fat 40g, saturated fat 23g, fibre 2g, sugar 38g, salt 0.97g

Whisked sponges are famously low in fat – especially if you use yogurt instead of cream as the filling. If you like, swap the fruit for whatever's in season.

Mango and passion fruit roulade

3 eggs
85g/3oz golden caster sugar, plus 1 tbsp
85g/3oz plain flour, sifted
1 tsp baking powder, sifted
1 tsp vanilla extract

FOR THE FILLING
1 tbsp golden caster sugar
flesh from 2 large ripe passion fruit
2 mangoes, peeled and cut into small chunks
250g pack frozen raspberries, defrosted
200g carton 2% Greek yogurt or very low-fat fromage frais

Takes 50 minutes, plus defrosting
Serves 10

1 Preheat the oven to 200°C/fan 180°C/gas 6. Grease and line a 30x23cm/12x9in Swiss roll tin. Put the eggs and sugar into a large bowl and beat with an electric mixer until thick and light, about 5 minutes. Fold in the flour and baking powder, then the vanilla. Tip into the tin, level the mix, then bake for 12–15 minutes or until golden and just springy. Turn out on to another sheet of paper, dusted with one tablespoon of caster sugar. Roll the paper up inside the sponge, then cool completely.

2 Fold the sugar, passion-fruit pulp and one-third of the mango and raspberries into the yogurt. Unroll the sponge, discard the paper and spread with the filling, then roll up again. Serve with the rest of the fruit on the side.

• Per slice 153 kcalories, protein 5g, carbohydrate 28g, fat 3g, saturated fat 1g, fibre 2g, sugar 21g, salt 0.26g

Why have one chocolate when you can have two? Go for all-out indulgence with these gooey, moreish marbled brownies.

Marbled chocolate brownies

200g/8oz plain chocolate (70% cocoa solids)
200g/8oz good-quality white chocolate
250g pack unsalted butter, cut into cubes
300g/10oz golden caster sugar
4 eggs, beaten
140g/5oz plain flour

Takes 50 minutes • Makes 16

1 Butter and line a 23cm/9in square brownie tin. Preheat the oven to 180°C/fan 160°C/gas 4. Put the plain and white chocolate into two bowls and add half of the butter to each. Heat over simmering water until the chocolate and butter are both melted. Stir well.
2 Add 150g/5½oz sugar and two beaten eggs to each bowl and beat until smooth. Now stir 50g/2oz of the flour into the plain chocolate mix and the remainder into the white mix.
3 Spoon tablespoons of the batter into the tin, alternating plain and white chocolate to create a patchwork pattern. Repeat, spooning white on top of the dark blobs, and vice-versa. Pull a skewer through the mix to make swirls.
4 Bake for 40–50 minutes or until the middle is just set and the white-chocolate patches have a pale golden crust. Cool in the tin before cutting.

• Per brownie 379 kcalories, protein 5g, carbohydrate 40g, fat 24g, saturated fat 14g, fibre 1g, sugar 31g, salt 0.09g

For big celebrations this cake is a must: four layers of moist sponge, lashings of chocolate ganache and the crunch of mouthwatering Maltesers.

White and dark chocolate cake

175g/6oz butter, softened, plus extra for greasing
100g/4oz white chocolate (choose a brand with real vanilla flecks)
100g/4oz plain chocolate (70% cocoa solids)
3 eggs
100ml/3½fl oz whole or semi-skimmed milk
175g/6oz caster sugar
1 tsp baking powder
200g/8oz self-raising flour
2 tbsp very strong coffee (instant is fine)
1 tsp vanilla extract

FOR THE GANACHE AND TO DECORATE
284ml carton double cream
200g/8oz plain chocolate (70% cocoa solids), broken into pieces
50g/2oz white chocolate, melted
1 small bag white Maltesers

Takes 1 hour, plus decorating • Serves 12

1 Preheat the oven to 180°C/fan 160°C/gas 4. Butter and line two 20cm/8in sandwich tins.
2 For the cake, break the chocolates into two separate bowls. Melt over simmering water. Put everything else, except the coffee and vanilla, into a bowl and beat until creamy.
3 Divide the mixture between two bowls, add the coffee and plain chocolate to one, and the vanilla and white chocolate to the other. Stir until mixed through then spoon into the tins. Level, then bake for 25 minutes or until risen and springy. Cool on a wire rack.
4 For the ganache, bring the cream to the boil. Pour over the plain chocolate and leave for 5 minutes. Stir until smooth, let it thicken and cool. Split the cakes horizontally across the middle, then layer up with the ganache.
5 To decorate, zigzag the white chocolate over the top of the cake, then finish with the Maltesers. Delicious served with pouring cream.

• Per slice 565 kcalories, protein 7g, carbohydrate 51g, fat 39g, saturated fat 22g, fibre 1g, sugar 37g, salt 0.62g

This cake is a real crowd-pleaser – moist, chocolatey and totally indulgent!

Orange and white chocolate sponge

175g/6oz butter, softened, plus extra for greasing
175g/6oz golden caster sugar
zest of 4 oranges and juice of 1
4 eggs, separated
100g/4oz self-raising flour
1 tsp baking powder
100g/4oz ground almonds

FOR THE ICING
200g/8oz white chocolate
200ml carton crème fraîche
chocolate curls, to serve (optional)

Takes 1 hour 10 minutes • Serves 10

1 Preheat the oven to 180°C/fan 160°C/gas 4. Butter and line two 20cm/8in sandwich tins. Beat the sugar, butter and orange zest until pale and fluffy, then beat in the egg yolks. Sift in the flour and baking powder, then fold in lightly. Fold in the almonds and the orange juice. Whisk the egg whites until they just hold their shape. Fold them into the batter in three lots, taking care not to over-mix.
2 Divide the mix between the tins and bake for 30–35 minutes. Cool in the tin for 5 minutes, then cool completely on a wire rack.
3 For the icing, melt the chocolate over a pan of barely simmering water, then leave to cool. Whip the crème fraîche until thick, then fold in the melted chocolate. Sandwich and top the cake with the icing and chill for at least 1 hour. Top with chocolate curls, if using.

• Per slice 567 kcalories, protein 9g, carbohydrate 45g, fat 40g, saturated fat 21g, fibre 1g, sugar 37g, salt 0.7g

These generous cupcakes will be a hit with kids and grown-ups alike and are ideal for a birthday party or other celebration.

Easy chocolate drop cakes

150ml carton natural yogurt
3 eggs, beaten
1 tsp vanilla extract
175g/6oz golden caster sugar
140g/5oz self-raising flour, minus
1 tbsp
1 tbsp cocoa powder
1 tsp baking powder
100g/4oz ground almonds
pinch of salt
175g/6oz unsalted butter, melted
12 chocolate buttons (optional), to decorate

FOR THE CHOCOLATE FROSTING
100g/4oz plain chocolate
140g/5oz unsalted butter
140g/5oz icing sugar

Takes 30 minutes • Makes 12 large or 24 small

1 Line a 12-hole muffin tin or two 12-hole bun tins with paper cases and preheat the oven to 190°C/fan 170°C/gas 5. Mix the yogurt, eggs and vanilla extract. Put the dry ingredients into a large bowl and make a well in the middle.

2 Add the yogurty mix and the melted butter, and quickly fold in using a spatula or metal spoon – don't overwork it. Spoon the mixture into the cases (they will be quite full) then bake for 18–20 minutes, if you're making the larger cakes, 12–15 minutes if you're making smaller ones, or until risen and springy to the touch. Cool for a few minutes, then lift the cakes on to a wire rack to cool completely.

3 Beat the frosting ingredients together until smooth, spread on to the cakes then top with a chocolate button, if using.

• Per large cupcake (with button) 492 kcalories, protein 6g, carbohydrate 47g, fat 32g, saturated fat 17g, fibre 1g, sugar 38g, salt 0.32g

This is a fantastic cake to serve as a dessert or at teatime over the festive season. Better still, it can be made up to a day in advance.

Dark chocolate and cranberry roulade

1 tbsp plain flour, for dusting
50g/2oz self-raising flour
1 tsp baking powder
25g/1oz good-quality cocoa powder, sifted
50g/2oz ground almonds
5 eggs
100g/4oz caster sugar, plus extra for turning the cake out

FOR THE FILLING
2 × 250g cartons mascarpone
zest of 1 orange
300g jar good-quality cranberry sauce (or use homemade)

FOR THE FROSTING
175g/6oz unsalted butter, softened
50g/2oz icing sugar, sifted
200g/8oz good-quality plain chocolate, melted and cooled

TO DECORATE
cranberries and bay leaves (optional)
icing sugar, to dust

Takes 1 hour 10 minutes, plus cooling
Serves 10

1 Preheat the oven to 190°C/fan 170°C/gas 5. Butter and line a 30x40cm/12x16in Swiss roll tin, then butter the parchment, dust with the plain flour and tip out any excess.
2 Mix the self-raising flour, baking powder, cocoa and almonds. Beat the eggs and sugar for 7–10 minutes until pale and thick. Fold in the dry ingredients. Pour into the tin then bake for 12–15 minutes or until firm.
3 Cool for 1 minute, then turn out on to a sheet of sugared non-stick baking paper. Remove the lining paper and roll the sponge up, short edge facing you, rolling the baking paper inside. Cool.
4 Beat the mascarpone with the orange zest. Unroll the sponge and spread with the mascarpone, leaving a border. Cover with the cranberry sauce. Roll it up again, tightly.
5 For the frosting, beat the butter and icing sugar until pale and then stir in the chocolate. Leave to firm up for 20 minutes then spread over the roulade. Finish with sugar-coated cranberries and bay leaves. Keep chilled until ready to serve.

• Per slice 691 kcalories, protein 9g, carbohydrate 48g, fat 52g, saturated fat 29g, fibre 2g, sugar 26g, salt 0.45g

Chocolate cakes and bakes

You'll be amazed how simple it is to make your own macaroons. Mini versions make delicious petits fours after dinner.

Coconut and chocolate macaroons

1 egg white
200g/8oz caster sugar
4 tbsp plain flour
200g/8oz coarsely grated fresh coconut (about 1 coconut in total)
150g bar plain chocolate (70% cocoa solids), chopped

Takes 40 minutes • Makes 12

1 Preheat the oven to 180°C/fan 160°C/ gas 4. In a clean bowl, whisk the egg white until stiff then gradually add the sugar, whisking continuously until thick and glossy. Sift in the flour and fold into the egg white with the coconut until completely combined.
2 Squash spoonfuls of the mixture on to a baking sheet lined with non-stick baking paper. (You may need to do this in two batches.) Bake for 15–18 minutes or until golden around the edges and just starting to brown on top. If you're making mini macaroons, check them after 10 minutes. Leave to cool. Transfer to a wire rack.
3 While the macaroons are cooling, melt the chocolate in a microwave or over a pan of simmering water and leave to cool slightly. Cover the smooth side of the macaroons with chocolate and leave to set in the fridge.

• Per macaroon 206 kcalories, protein 2g, carbohydrate 30g, fat 10g, saturated fat 7g, fibre 2g, sugar 26g, salt 0.03g

Whether you are using lurid colours for a psychedelic finish, or just swirling chocolate and vanilla batter, making marble cake seems to bring memories flooding back.

Chocolate marble cake

225g/8oz butter, softened
225g /8oz caster sugar
4 eggs
225g/8oz self-raising flour
3 tbsp milk
1 tsp vanilla extract
2 tbsp cocoa powder

Takes 1 hour 10 minutes • Serves 8

1 Preheat the oven to 180°C/fan 160°C/ gas 4. Grease and line a round 20cm/8in tin. Beat the butter and sugar together, then add the eggs, one at a time, mixing well after each addition. Fold through the flour, milk and vanilla extract until the mixture is smooth.
2 Divide the mixture between two bowls. Stir the cocoa powder into the mixture in one of the bowls. Dollop the chocolate and vanilla cake mixes into the tin alternately. When all the mixture has been used up, tap the bottom to remove any air bubbles. Then take a skewer and swirl it around the mixture in the tin a few times to create a marbled effect.
3 Bake the cake for 45–55 minutes or until a skewer inserted into the centre comes out clean. Turn out on to a wire rack and leave to cool.

• Per slice 468 kcalories, protein 6g, carbohydrate 52g, fat 27g, saturated fat 16g, fibre 1g, sugar 31g, salt 0.81g

The subtle combination of chocolate and spices makes these blissful bites a heavenly treat.

Crumbly cinnamon and chocolate squares

175g/6oz butter at room temperature, cubed
200g/8oz golden caster sugar
175g/6oz plain flour
3 eggs
3 tbsp milk
1 tsp baking powder

FOR THE TOPPING
100g/4oz plain chocolate, roughly chopped
1 tsp ground cinnamon
100g/4oz light muscovado sugar
85g/3oz chopped mixed nuts

Takes 1 hour 10 minutes • Makes 15

1 Preheat the oven to 180°C/fan 160°C/ gas 4. Line the base of an 18x27cm/ 7x11in tin with greaseproof paper. Put the cake ingredients into a large mixing bowl, then beat with an electric hand mixer until well blended and creamy.

2 Tip the mixture into the cake tin, spread evenly right into the corners, then scatter the chocolate on top. Mix the remaining topping ingredients and scatter over the top of the chocolate. Lightly press to compact the mixture, then bake for 40 minutes or until risen and firm to the touch. Cool in the tin before cutting into squares.

• Per square 294 kcalories, protein 4g, carbohydrate 35g, fat 16g, saturated fat 8g, fibre 1g, added sugar 25g, salt 0.39g

A pure, unadulterated chocolate hit that is made extra special with the addition of crunchy hazelnut praline.

Chocolate and hazelnut praline tart

140g/5oz butter
100g/4oz golden caster sugar
225g/8oz plain flour
50g/2oz ground almonds
1 egg, beaten

FOR THE FILLING
50g/2oz golden caster sugar
85g/3oz blanched hazelnuts, toasted
200g/8oz plain chocolate
(70% cocoa solids)
100g/4oz butter
splash of Frangelico-hazelnut liqueur
or brandy
1 egg
3 egg yolks

Takes 1 hour • Serves 10

1 Cream the butter and sugar. Add flour and almonds. Bring together with the egg. Chill for 20 minutes. Roll to fit a 23cm/9in fluted flan tin leave a slight overhang. Chill for 20 minutes.
2 Preheat the oven to 200°C/fan 180°C/gas 6. Blind-bake the case for 10 minutes then remove the baking beans and cook for another 10 minutes or until golden.
3 Heat four tablespoons of the sugar in a non-stick pan until it caramelizes. Add the nuts. Tip out on to an oiled baking sheet. Cool, then roughly chop. Melt the chocolate, butter and alcohol together. Beat the egg, yolks and remaining sugar in a bowl over a pan of simmering water until pale and fluffy. Fold in the chocolate mix off the heat.
4 When the pastry is cooked, turn the oven down to 160°C/fan 140°C/gas 3. Scatter most of the nuts over the base. Tip in the chocolate mix, pressing down slightly. Cook for 15–20 minutes until almost set. Decorate with the rest of the nuts.

• Per slice 582 kcalories, protein 9g, carbohydrate 50g, fat 40g, saturated fat 18g, fibre 3g, sugar 29g, salt 0.43g

Indulge yourself with this moist and fudgy chocolate cake – it's perfect for birthdays, weddings, christenings, or any other celebration. Any excuse will do!

Ultimate chocolate cake

200g/8oz butter, cut into pieces
200g/8oz plain chocolate (about 60% cocoa solids), chopped
1 tbsp instant coffee granules
85g/3oz self-raising flour
85g/3oz plain flour
¼ tsp bicarbonate of soda
200g/8oz light muscovado sugar
200g/8oz golden caster sugar
25g/1oz cocoa powder
3 medium eggs
5 tbsp buttermilk
grated chocolate or curls, to decorate

FOR THE GANACHE
284ml carton double cream
2 tbsp golden caster sugar
200g/8oz plain chocolate (as above), chopped

Takes about 2 hours • Serves 14

1 Butter and bottom-line a deep 20cm/8in round cake tin. Preheat the oven to 160°C/fan 140°C/gas 3. Put the butter, chocolate, coffee granules and 125ml/4fl oz of cold water into a pan and gently heat until melted.
2 Mix the flours, bicarbonate of soda, sugars and cocoa in a bowl. Beat the eggs with the buttermilk. Pour the chocolate and egg mixes into the flour mixture, stirring until smooth. Pour into the tin and bake for about 1½hours or until a skewer comes out clean. Cool in the tin then turn out on to a wire rack. Once cold, cut the cake horizontally into three.
3 Make the ganache. Bring the cream and sugar up to a boil in a pan then pour over the chocolate. Stir until smooth. Sandwich the layers together with a little ganache. Smooth the rest over the cake. Decorate with grated chocolate or a pile of chocolate curls.

• Per slice 541 kcalories, protein 6g, carbohydrate 55g, fat 35g, saturated fat 20g, fibre 2g, sugar 40g, salt 0.51g

If you like icecream sundaes, you're going to love this. When you get it out of the freezer, add your own personal touch with some sliced ripe banana or strawberries – or both.

Choc and nut sundae cake

85g/3oz butter, melted and cooled, plus extra for greasing
4 tbsp cocoa powder, plus 1 tsp, sifted
5 eggs
175g/6oz golden caster sugar
100g/4oz plain flour

FOR THE SAUCE
100g bar plain chocolate (70% cocoa solids)
50g/2oz butter
1 tbsp golden syrup
1 tbsp instant coffee granules
3 tbsp just-boiled water

FOR THE ICE CREAM AND TO DECORATE
2 × 500ml carton good-quality vanilla ice cream, softened for 5 minutes
4 Cadbury's Flake bars, crumbled
100g/4oz toasted hazelnuts, roughly chopped

Takes 45 minutes, plus cooling, freezing and defrosting • Serves 8

1 Preheat the oven to 190°C/fan 170°C/gas 5. Butter and line a 23cm/9in springform cake tin, then butter the lining. Coat with one teaspoon of cocoa, tapping out the excess.
2 Whisk the eggs and sugar for 5 minutes until thick and pale. Fold in the butter, then the flour and cocoa. Bake for 20 minutes or until risen and springy. Cool for 5 minutes then turn out on to a wire rack to cool.
3 Melt all the sauce ingredients together, stir, then set aside.
4 Cut the cake in half. Scoop one carton of ice cream evenly on to the base and top with half the Flake and hazelnuts. Sit the second piece of cake on top. Cover with remaining ice cream, chocolate and nuts. Serve with the sauce or freeze for up to 1 month. If frozen, transfer the cake to the fridge 1 hour before serving.

• Per slice 708 kcalories, protein 13g, carbohydrate 67g, fat 45g, saturated fat 22g, fibre 3g, sugar 53g, salt 0.58g

These brownies are just as they should be – intensely chocolatey and gooey in the middle and with a slight crust.

Best-ever brownies

200g/8oz butter
200g/8oz plain chocolate
175g/6oz dark muscovado sugar
140g/5oz granulated or caster sugar
4 eggs
50g/2oz ground almonds
50g/2oz plain flour

Takes 40 minutes • Makes 16

1 Preheat the oven to 180°C/fan 160°C/ gas 4, then grease and line a 20cm/8in square brownie tin. Heat the butter and chocolate in a pan until melted. Stir through the sugars.
2 Leave to cool for 5 minutes, then stir in the eggs until even. Mix in the almonds and flour then pour into the tin. Bake for 30–35 minutes or until just cooked through in the middle.

• Per brownie 287 kcalories, protein 3.6g, carbohydrate 31.3g, fat 17.2g, saturated fat 9.1g, fibre 0.6g, sugar 28.7g, salt 0.25g

Perfect for breakfast, coffee or afternoon tea, this Danish pastry is big enough to share and a pleasure to make.

Double chocolate Easter Danish

175ml/6fl oz warm milk
1 egg, beaten
450g/1lb strong white flour
1 sachet fast-action dried yeast
50g/2oz golden caster sugar
250g block cold butter, sliced
pinch of salt

FOR THE FILLING
200g/7oz flaked toasted almonds
50g/2oz icing sugar
25g/1oz cocoa powder
50g/2oz butter, softened
1 egg white
50g/2oz plain chocolate, chopped
into small pieces

FOR THE GLAZE
1 egg yolk, beaten with 3 tbsp milk
golden caster sugar, for sprinkling

FOR THE ICING
50g/2oz icing sugar

Takes 1½ hours, plus rising time
Serves 8

1 Beat the milk and egg together. Pulse the flour, yeast, sugar, butter and salt in a processor until the mix starts to come together. Tip into a bowl and use your hands to work in the liquid. Knead the dough slightly on a floured surface, then roll into a rectangle. Fold the top and bottom thirds into the middle. Repeat twice. Cover and chill for 4 hours.
2 Pulse 150g/5½oz of the almonds, icing sugar, cocoa, butter, egg white and chocolate to a paste. Halve the dough then press one piece into a buttered 23cm/9in springform tin. Spread the filling over, leaving a border, then top with remaining dough. Let it rise for 1 hour.
3 Preheat the oven to 180°C/fan 160°C/ gas 4. Brush the dough with the glaze, sprinkle with the remaining almonds and some sugar. Bake for 40–50 minutes or until golden. Cool. Mix the icing sugar with a little water and drizzle it over the cake.

• Per slice 654 kcalories, protein 5g, carbohydrate 52g, fat 49g, saturated fat 28g, fibre 2g, sugar 38g, salt 0.30g

Whole orange, cooked until tender then added, skin and all, gives this chocolate cake a wonderful moistness and bitter citrus flavour. Serve warm with a scoop of ice cream.

Whole orange and chocolate cake

1 small orange (about 200g/8oz)
100g/4oz self-raising flour
1 tsp baking powder
1 tsp ground cinnamon
1 tsp ground coriander
2 tbsp cocoa powder
100g/4oz ground almonds
175g/6oz butter, softened
175g/6oz light muscovado sugar
4 eggs, separated

Takes 2 hours 15 minutes • Serves 12

1 Butter and line the base of a 23cm/9in round tin. Put the orange in a pan and cover with water. Bring to the boil, then simmer, partly covered, for 1 hour. Drain and cool. Preheat the oven to 180°C/fan 160°C/gas 4.
2 Halve the orange, remove the pips, then chop (without peeling). Put in the food processor and work to a rough purée. Sift together the flour, baking powder, spices and cocoa. Stir in the ground almonds.
3 Beat the butter and sugar until light and fluffy. Beat in the egg yolks and the orange, then fold in the flour mix. Beat the egg whites until stiff, then fold gently into the cake mix in two batches. Pour into the prepared tin and bake for 40–45 minutes or until firm. Cool for 5 minutes in the tin, then turn out and cool on a wire rack.

• Per slice 285 kcalories, protein 5g, carbohydrate 24g, fat 19g, saturated fat 9g, fibre 1g, sugar 16g, salt 0.52g

A great marriage of two sweet classics, these cupcakes will disappear in no time.

Doughnut cupcakes

200g/8oz butter, softened, plus
3 tbsp, melted
200g/8oz sugar
2 eggs, plus 1 yolk
300g/10oz self-raising flour
100ml/3½fl oz milk
½ tsp baking powder
12 tsp strawberry jam (about ⅓ of
a jar)
3–4 sugar cubes, roughly crushed

Takes 40 minutes • Makes 12

1 Preheat the oven to 180°C/fan 160°C/ gas 4. Tip the softened butter, sugar, eggs and egg yolk, flour, milk and baking powder into a large bowl. Beat together until you have a smooth, soft batter.

2 Line a 12-hole tin with paper cases and fill the cases two-thirds full with the batter. Make a small dip in the batter in each and spoon in one teaspoon of jam. Cover with another tablespoon of cake batter and repeat for the remaining cupcakes. Bake in the oven for 25 minutes or until risen and cooked through.

3 Brush some melted butter over each cake, then sprinkle with the crushed sugar and serve. Will keep for up to 2 days in an airtight container.

• Per cupcake 363 kcalories, protein 4g, carbohydrate 47g, fat 19g, saturated fat 11g, fibre 1g, sugar 28g, salt 0.66g

The key to light muffins is quick mixing, but this recipe has a secret ingredient too – sparkling water. Once added, bake and watch them rise!

Blueberry, peach and soured cream muffins

350g/12oz self-raising flour
1 tsp baking powder
100g/4oz light muscovado sugar
100g/4oz butter, melted
142ml carton soured cream
2 medium eggs
zest of 1 lemon
150g punnet blueberries or blackberries
2 fresh peaches, stoned and cut into wedges
6 tbsp sparkling water
demerara sugar, to sprinkle

Takes 45–55 minutes • Makes 8

1 Preheat the oven to 200°C/fan 180°C/gas 6 and put eight muffin cases in a muffin tin. Mix the flour, baking powder and sugar in a large bowl, add the melted butter, soured cream, eggs and lemon zest, and beat just long enough to create a thick, smooth mixture – don't overbeat. Carefully stir in the fruit and, finally, the sparkling water, until evenly combined.
2 Divide the mixture among the muffin cases. (They should be nice and full.) Sprinkle generously with the sugar and bake for 25–30 minutes or until risen and golden. The muffins are best served just warm. They will keep fresh in an airtight container in a cool place for 1–2 days.

• Per muffin 360 kcalories, protein 7g, carbohydrate 50g, fat 16g, saturated fat 9g, fibre 3g, added sugar 13g, salt 0.9g

The beauty of these little cakes is in their simplicity – just a dollop of cream and a single raspberry turns a basic fairy cake into a chic little delicacy.

Glamorous fairy cakes

140g/5oz butter, very well softened
140g/5oz golden caster sugar
3 medium eggs
100g/4oz self-raising flour
25g/1oz custard powder or cornflour

TO DECORATE
mascarpone or whipped cream
1 punnet raspberries or blackberries
fresh mint leaves
1 tbsp icing sugar

Takes 45–55 minutes • Makes 24

1 Preheat the oven to 190°C/fan 170°C/ gas 5 and arrange paper cases in bun tins. Put all the cake ingredients in a large bowl and beat for about 2 minutes until smooth. Divide the mixture among the cases so they are half filled and bake for 12–15 minutes or until risen and golden. Cool on a wire rack.
2 Top each cake with a tablespoon of mascarpone or cream, a raspberry or blackberry and a mint leaf. Dust with icing sugar.

• Per cake 193 kcalories, protein 2g, carbohydrate 36g, fat 6g, saturated fat 3g, fibre none, added sugar 31g, salt 0.2g

These waist-watching muffins taste as good as they look. To keep them delicious and low fat the mixture relies on the sweetness of the bananas, so use the ripest ones you can find.

Banana and blueberry muffins

300g/10oz self-raising flour
1 tsp bicarbonate of soda
100g/4oz light muscovado sugar
50g/2oz porridge oats, plus 1 tbsp
for topping
2 medium bananas (the riper
the better)
284ml carton buttermilk (or use mild
natural yogurt)
5 tbsp light olive oil
2 egg whites
150g punnet blueberries

Takes 35 minutes • Makes 12

1 Preheat the oven to 180°C/fan 160°C/gas 4 and line a 12-hole muffin tin with paper cases. Tip the flour and bicarbonate of soda into a large bowl. Hold back one tablespoon of the sugar, then mix the remainder with the flour and the oats.

2 In a separate bowl, mash the bananas until nearly smooth. Stir the buttermilk, oil and egg whites into the banana until even.

3 Make a well in the centre of the flour mix, pour in the wet mix and stir quickly and sparingly. (It will look lumpy, but don't be tempted to over-mix.) Tip in the blueberries and give it just one more stir.

4 Divide among the muffin cases (they will be quite full), then sprinkle with the remaining oats and sugar. Bake for 18–20 minutes or until risen and dark golden. Cool for 5 minutes in the tin before lifting out on to a wire rack to cool.

• Per muffin 202 kcalories, protein 5g, carbohydrate 36g, fat 5g, saturated fat 0.8g, fibre 2g, sugar 14g, salt 0.59g

Although fruity, these lunchbox-friendly muffins aren't too sweet and are delicious eaten with a slice of cheese.

Apple pecan muffins

350g/12oz plain flour
25g/1oz butter
50g/2oz dark muscovado sugar, plus
1 tbsp for the topping
50g/2oz pecan nuts, chopped
2 tsp baking powder
½ tsp bicarbonate of soda
pinch of salt
1 tsp ground cinnamon
3 eating apples (about 140g/5oz
each), peeled and cored
284ml carton soured cream
1 egg, beaten
3 tbsp milk

Takes 30 minutes • Makes 12

1 Preheat the oven to 200°C/fan 180°C/gas 6. Line a 12-hole muffin tin with cases. To make the topping, rub 50g/2oz of the flour with the butter to make breadcrumbs. Stir through one tablespoon of sugar and the chopped pecans.

2 In a large bowl, sift together the remaining flour, baking powder, bicarbonate of soda and salt. Stir in the sugar and cinnamon and set aside. Coarsely grate two apples, then beat together with the soured cream, egg and milk. Make a well in the dry ingredients and quickly fold through the wet ingredients.

3 Spoon the mixture into the muffin cases and sprinkle over the topping. Thinly slice the last apple and poke slices into the muffin tops. Bake for 20 minutes or until golden and a skewer inserted comes out clean.

• Per muffin 226 kcalories, protein 5g, carbohydrate 32g, fat 9g, saturated fat 5g, fibre 2g, sugar 9g, salt 0.56g

This storecupboard staple is perfect for unexpected guests – you can have a batch of scones on the table in 20 minutes.

Classic scones with jam and clotted cream

350g/12oz self-raising flour, plus more for dusting
¼ tsp salt
1 tsp baking powder
85g/3oz cold butter, cut into cubes
3 tbsp caster sugar
175ml/6fl oz milk, warmed
1 tsp vanilla extract
squeeze of fresh lemon juice
1 beaten egg, to glaze
jam and clotted cream, to serve

Takes 20 minutes • Makes 8

1 Preheat the oven to 220°C/fan 200°C/gas 7 and put a baking sheet in the oven. Mix the flour, salt and baking powder in a large bowl. Rub in the butter until the mixture looks like fine crumbs. Stir in the sugar. Make a well in the centre.

2 Combine the milk, vanilla and lemon juice then pour it into the dry mixture. Mix with a cutlery knife – it will seem quite wet. Tip the dough out on to a lightly floured surface. Dredge the dough and your hands with flour. Fold the dough over 2 or 3 times until it's a little smoother. Pat into a round about 4cm/13/4in deep.

3 Take a plain 5cm/2in cutter and dip it into some flour. Cut out four scones. Press what's left back into a round and repeat. Brush the scone tops with egg. Place on the hot sheet. Bake for 10 minutes or until risen and golden.

• Per scone 268 kcalories, protein 6g, carbohydrate 41g, fat 10g, saturated fat 6g, fibre 1g, sugar 8g, salt 0.95g

Butterfly cakes are perfect for making with children, and this blueberry and lemon version is a good way to encourage them to eat fruit.

Blueberry butterfly cakes

140g/5oz self-raising flour
½ tsp baking powder
85g/3oz butter, at room temperature
85g/3oz golden caster sugar
50g/2oz lemon curd
2 eggs
100g/4oz blueberries

FOR THE TOPPING
175g/6oz reduced-fat Mascarpone
50g/2oz lemon curd
100g/4oz blueberries
icing sugar, for dusting

Takes 40 minutes • Makes 12

1 Preheat the oven to 180°C/160°C fan/gas 4 and line a 12-hole bun tin with cases. Put the flour, baking powder, butter, sugar, lemon curd and eggs into a large bowl. Beat until creamy using an electric hand mixer then carefully stir in the blueberries.
2 Spoon the mixture evenly into the paper cases, then bake for 15 minutes or until the cakes are golden and risen. Cool for a few minutes, then lift the cakes on to a wire rack. While they cool, make the topping by beating the mascarpone and lemon curd together.
3 Carefully cut a circle out of the top of each cake, lift it off and fill the space with the lemon topping, followed by some blueberries. Halve each cake circle and poke them into the topping at an angle. Dust with icing sugar and serve.

• Per cake 206 kcalories, protein 3g, carbohydrate 23g, fat 12g, saturated fat 7g, fibre 1g, sugar 13g, salt 0.37g

Rhubarb is cleverly combined with custard as a surprise filling for these light muffins. For best results, buy really thick custard.

Rhubarb and custard muffins

300g/10oz rhubarb, cut into 3cm/
1in lengths
50g/2oz caster sugar
140g/5oz light muscovado sugar
75ml/2½fl oz vegetable oil
1 egg
zest of 1 orange
284ml carton soured cream
300g/10oz self-raising flour
8 tbsp ready-made thick Devon
custard (from a carton), chilled
caster sugar, for sprinkling

Takes 40 minutes, plus roasting the
rhubarb • Makes 12

1 Preheat the oven to 200°C/fan 180°C/ gas 6. Put the rhubarb in a roasting tin, toss with the caster sugar, then cover with foil. Roast for 15 minutes. Uncover, stir and roast for 5 minutes more until tender. Cool, then drain.
2 Lower the oven to 180°C/fan 160°C/ gas 4. Line a 12-hole muffin tin with cases. Beat together the muscovado sugar, oil, egg, zest and soured cream until combined. Gently mix in the flour. Fold in the rhubarb.
3 Divide three-quarters of the batter evenly among the cases. Using a spoon, press the centre of each muffin to make a dip. Fill each dip with a small blob of custard. Gently cover with the rest of the muffin mix. Bake for 25 minutes or until risen, pale golden and oozing. Sprinkle each with a little caster sugar while still warm. Eat on the day of baking.

• Per muffin 266 kcalories, protein 4g, carbohydrate 38g, fat 12g, saturated fat 4g, fibre 1g, added sugar 18g, salt 0.30g

Pice ar y Maen are a Welsh teatime treat that have been passed down through generations and are still as popular as ever. Serve them buttered and hot, straight from the griddle.

Welsh cakes

225g/8oz plain flour
85g/3oz caster sugar plus a little extra, for dusting
½ tsp mixed spice
½ tsp baking powder
pinch of salt
50g/2oz cold butter, cut into small pieces
50g/2oz cold lard, cut into small pieces, plus extra for frying
50g/2oz currants
1 egg, beaten
splash of milk

Takes 15 minutes • Makes 16

1 Tip the flour, sugar, mixed spice, baking powder and salt into a bowl. Then, using your fingers, rub in the butter and lard until crumbly. Mix in the currants. Work the egg into the mixture until you have soft dough, adding a splash of milk if it seems a little dry – it should be the same consistency as pastry.
2 Roll out the dough on a lightly floured work surface to the thickness of your little finger. Cut out rounds using a 6cm/2½in cutter, re-rolling any trimmings. Grease a flat griddle pan or heavy frying pan with lard, then place over a medium heat. Cook the Welsh cakes in batches, for about 3 minutes each side, until golden brown, crisp and cooked through. Delicious served warm with butter and jam, or simply sprinkled with caster sugar.

• Per cake 138 kcalories, protein 2g, carbohydrate 20g, fat 6g, saturated fat 1g, fibre 9g, sugar 9g, salt 0.13g

If you're not keen on cherries, swap them for the same quantity of chopped, ready-to-eat dried apricots or raisins.

Choc-cherry muffins

250g/9oz self-raising flour
1 tsp bicarbonate of soda
140g/5oz dried sour cherries
100g bar white chocolate, cut into chunks
100g bar plain chocolate, cut into chunks
100g/4oz golden caster sugar
2 eggs, beaten
150ml carton natural yogurt
100g/4oz butter, melted

Takes 35 minutes • Makes 12

1 Preheat the oven to 200°C/fan 180°C/gas 6 and line a 12-hole muffin tin with paper cases. Sift the flour and bicarbonate of soda into a large bowl, then stir in the cherries, both chocolates and sugar. Add the beaten eggs and yogurt, and then the butter, and stir to combine. It doesn't matter if the mixture looks a bit lumpy, it's more important not to over mix or the muffins will turn out tough.
2 Fill the paper cases and bake for 20–25 minutes or until risen and golden brown. Transfer to a wire rack to cool. They are especially delicious eaten slightly warm.

• Per muffin 386 kcalories, protein 5g, carbohydrate 45g, fat 13g, saturated fat 6g, fibre 1g, added sugar 18g, salt 0.73g

These fruity pancakes are perfect for a leisurely brunch and are healthier than most bought versions too.

Apricot pancakes with honey butter

FOR THE BUTTER
100g/4oz butter, softened
2 tbsp clear honey

FOR THE PANCAKES
140g/5oz self-raising flour
pinch of bicarbonate of soda
pinch of salt
25g/1oz caster sugar
1 egg
150ml/5fl oz milk
handful of ready-to-eat dried apricots, finely chopped
vegetable or sunflower oil, for frying

Takes 15 minutes, plus chilling
Serves 4

1 For the honey butter, beat the butter with the honey and spoon on to a large piece of cling film. Squeeze into a sausage shape, then wrap tightly and chill until ready to use. Will keep in the fridge for up to a month.
2 To make the pancakes, sift the flour, bicarbonate of soda and salt into a bowl, then stir through the sugar and make a well in the centre. Beat together the egg and milk, then gradually pour into the well, stirring slowly, to avoid creating lumps. Stir in the apricots.
3 Heat a non-stick frying pan over a low heat and add a little oil. Drop in four tablespoons of batter and cook for 1 minute or until the surface of each pancake is covered in bubbles. Flip with a palette knife or fish slice, then cook for a further minute. Repeat with the remaining batter. Serve warm with the honey butter.

• Per pancake 406 kcalories, protein 7g, carbohydrate 45g, fat 23g, saturated fat 14g, fibre 2g, sugar 19g, salt 1.23g

You'll have some clotted cream left over if you make only twelve cakes, but it's not hard to find a reason to finish off the pot!

Clotted cream splits

150ml carton natural yogurt
3 eggs, beaten
1 tsp vanilla extract
175g/6oz golden caster sugar
140g/5oz self-raising flour
1 tsp baking powder
100g/4oz ground almonds
pinch of salt
175g/6oz unsalted butter, melted

TO SERVE
jar of raspberry jam
100g/4oz raspberries
550g carton clotted cream
icing sugar, to dust

Takes 30 minutes • Makes 12

1 Line a 12-hole muffin tin with paper cases and preheat the oven to 190°C/fan 170°C/gas 5. In a jug, mix the yogurt, eggs and vanilla extract. Put the dry ingredients into a large bowl and make a well in the middle.
2 Pour in the yogurty mix and melted butter and quickly fold in with a spatula or metal spoon – don't overwork it. Spoon the mixture into the cases (they will be quite full) and bake for 18–20 minutes or until risen and springy to the touch. Cool for a few minutes, then lift the cakes on to a wire rack to cool completely.
3 Cut the tops off the cupcakes and set aside. Spoon a dollop of raspberry jam on to each one and top with a few raspberries and generously heaped teaspoons of clotted cream. Put the tops back on, then dust with icing sugar to serve.

• Per split 378 kcalories, protein 6g, carbohydrate 32g, fat 26g, saturated fat 13g, fibre 1g, sugar 23g, salt 0.33g

For a fresh start to the day, serve a stack of American pancakes instead of a cooked breakfast – but beware, one is never enough!

American-style pineapple and banana pancakes

100g/4oz fresh or canned pineapple (drained, if canned)
1 banana
100g/4oz self-raising flour
1 tsp baking powder
1 tsp ground cinnamon
3 tbsp light muscovado sugar
1 egg
100ml/3½fl oz milk
sunflower oil, for frying
Greek yogurt and maple syrup, to serve

Takes 20 minutes • Serves 4

1 Roughly chop the pineapple and slice the banana. Tip the flour, baking powder, cinnamon and sugar into a bowl and mix well. Make a well into the centre and crack in the egg, then mix it into the flour a little at a time, adding the milk gradually to make a soft batter. Stir in the pineapple and banana.

2 Heat a little oil in a non-stick frying pan, add the batter in heaped tablespoons well apart to allow them to spread. When bubbles appear on the surface, flip the pancakes over and cook until light golden. Cook all the pancakes and keep them warm. Serve 2–3 pancakes with a spoonful of yogurt and a little maple syrup poured over.

• Per pancake 230 kcalories, protein 6g, carbohydrate 42g, fat 6g, saturated fat 1g, fibre 1g, sugar 11g, salt 0.7g

Strawberries and cream is always a winning combination, but it is especially so on these decadent summer shortcakes. The bases are a little like scones, but lighter and crisper around the edges.

Strawberry vanilla shortcakes

350g/12oz self-raising flour, plus extra for dusting
100g/4oz butter, cold and cubed
100g/4oz caster sugar
1 vanilla pod, seeds scraped and reserved
1/4 tsp salt
100ml/3½fl oz milk, warmed
1 egg, plus a little extra beaten egg to glaze
squeeze of fresh lemon juice

FOR THE TOPPING
227g carton clotted cream
strawberry jam
250g/9oz strawberries, thickly sliced

Takes 30 minutes • Makes 8

1 Preheat the oven to 220°C/fan 200°C/gas 7. Lightly flour a baking sheet. Put the flour, butter, sugar, half the vanilla seeds and the salt into a processor and pulse until fine. Tip into a large bowl. Beat the milk, egg and lemon juice together, tip into the dry mix and bring to a clumpy dough using a cutlery knife.
2 Lightly flour the work surface then shape the dough into a smoothish disc. Cut out eight rounds using a 7cm/3in cutter (you'll need to pinch together the trimmings). Glaze the tops only with the beaten egg, lift on to the baking sheet and bake for 10–12 minutes or until risen and golden. Cool on a wire rack.
3 Beat the remaining vanilla seeds into the cream (it will go runny then get thicker again). Cut the very top off each shortcake and top with jam, the flavoured cream and a mound of strawberries.

• Per shortcake 502 kcalories, protein 6g, carbohydrate 55g, fat 30g, saturated fat 18g, fibre 2g, sugar 22g, salt 0.82g

Quick and easy to make using storecupboard ingredients, these griddle scones are delicious eaten with honey and butter for afternoon tea.

Griddle scones with honey

200g/8oz self-raising flour
¼ tsp ground cardamom (about 10 pods, ground)
25g/1oz cold butter, cubed
25g/1oz light muscovado sugar
1 egg
about 5 tbsp milk
butter and honey, to serve

Takes 15 minutes • Makes 12

1 Put the flour and cardamom in a bowl and rub in the butter. Add the sugar. Beat the egg in a measuring jug, then pour in the milk to make it up to 100ml/3½fl oz. Pour into the bowl gradually, stirring first with a knife and then with your hands, to make a soft, not sticky, dough. Knead until smooth on a floured work surface.

2 Divide the dough into three and roll into circles the thickness of a £1 coin. Cut each into quarters. Heat a heavy-bottomed frying pan to medium hot. Cook the scones in batches for a couple of minutes each side, until golden brown. Serve spread with butter and drizzled with honey.

• Per scone 90 kcalories, protein 2g, carbohydrate 15g, fat 3g, saturated fat 1g, fibre 1g, sugar 2g, salt 0.22g

Not everyone likes fruit cake at Christmas, so why not make these vanilla cupcakes instead, topped with a snowy mallow festive frosting.

Snow-capped fairy cakes

175g/6oz butter
175g/6oz golden caster sugar
3 eggs
200g/8oz self-raising flour
zest of 1 orange
1 tsp vanilla extract
4 tbsp milk

FOR THE FROSTING
1 egg white
4 tbsp fresh orange juice
175g/6oz icing sugar
silver balls and jelly diamonds, to decorate

Takes 30 minutes • Makes 18

1 Preheat the oven to 190°C/fan 170°C/gas 5. Line 18 holes of two 12-hole bun tins with cases. Melt the butter and cool for 5 minutes, then tip into a large bowl with all the cake ingredients. Beat together until smooth.
2 Spoon the cake mixture into the cake cases, filling them three-quarters full. Bake for 15–18 minutes or until lightly browned and firm to the touch. Cool on a wire rack.
3 To make the frosting, put the egg white and orange juice into a heatproof bowl, sift in the icing sugar, then set over a pan of simmering water. Using an electric hand whisk, whisk the icing for 7 minutes or until it is glossy and stands in soft peaks. Whisk for a further 2 minutes off the heat.
4 Swirl the frosting on to the cakes then decorate with jelly diamonds and a few silver balls. Leave to set.

• Per cake 210 kcalories, protein 3g, carbohydrate 31g, fat 9g, saturated fat 5g, fibre none, sugar 22g, salt 0.31g

Kids will love helping with these cute cupcakes. They're perfect for serving at Easter, but equally delicious at any time of the year.

Easter egg cupcakes

250g pack butter, softened, plus extra for greasing
175g/6oz golden caster sugar
5 eggs, beaten
250g/9oz self-raising flour, plus an extra 2 tbsp
1 tsp baking powder
zest of 1 orange, plus 2 tbsp of the juice
200g/8oz glacé cherries, chopped
250g/9oz natural marzipan, coarsely grated (easiest if chilled beforehand)
½ tsp almond essence, optional

TO DECORATE
100g/4oz icing sugar
chocolate mini eggs

Takes 40 minutes • Makes 24

1 Preheat the oven to 180°C/fan 160°C/gas 4 and butter and line two 12-hole bun tins with paper cases. Beat the butter and sugar until light and fluffy. Add the eggs, 250g/9oz flour, baking powder, orange zest and juice, and beat well until creamy and even.

2 Toss the cherries in the extra flour and fold into the batter along with the grated marzipan and almond essence (if using). Spoon into the cases and bake for 20–25 minutes or until well risen and golden. Cool.

3 Mix the icing sugar with just over one tablespoon of water to make a loose icing, spoon over the cupcakes, then fix a few chocolate mini eggs on top of each.

• Per cupcake 281 kcalories, protein 3.7g, carbohydrate 38.7g, fat 13.4g, saturated fat 6.1g, fibre 0.6g, sugar 30g, salt 0.41g

Who could resist a pretty pile of these colourful, fruitful cupcakes?

Raspberry cupcakes with orange drizzle

200g/8oz self-raising flour
2 tsp baking powder
200g/8oz unsalted butter, softened
4 eggs
200g/8oz caster sugar
3 tbsp milk
50g/2oz ground almonds
zest of 1 medium orange
150g punnet raspberries, lightly
crushed, plus extra to decorate

FOR THE ORANGE DRIZZLE
juice of 1 medium orange
4 tbsp caster sugar

Takes 35 minutes • Makes 12

1 Preheat the oven to 180°C/fan 160°C/
gas 4. Line a 12-hole muffin tin with paper
cases. Tip the first eight ingredients into
a large bowl and beat with an electric
hand whisk until smooth. Fold the crushed
raspberries through the batter.
2 Divide the batter among the cases (they
should be about half full) and bake for
20–25 minutes or until golden and just firm.
3 Make the orange drizzle topping by mixing
together the orange juice and sugar until
well blended.
4 Remove the cupcakes from the oven and
allow to cool a little. Drizzle each with the
orange mix. Top with the extra raspberries to
serve.

• Per cupcake 328 kcalories, protein 5g, carbohydrate
37g, fat 19g, saturated fat 10g, fibre 1g, sugar 23g,
salt 0.49g

This zingy tart has a wonderful flavour and is a great way to cook with passion fruit.

Caramelized passion fruit and lime tart

500g pack dessert pastry
8 passion fruit
finely grated zest and juice of 1 lime
200g/8oz golden caster sugar
6 egg yolks
142ml carton double cream
icing sugar, for dusting (optional)

Takes 1 hour 15 minutes, plus cooling
Serves 8

1 Roll out the pastry and line a 23cm/9in tart case, then chill for at least 20 minutes. Preheat the oven to 180°C/fan 160°C/gas 4. Line the tart with baking parchment and baking beans, then bake for 15 minutes. Remove the parchment, bake for a further 5–10 minutes or until golden, then remove from the oven and turn it down to 140°C/fan 120°C/gas 1.

2 Cut the passion fruit in half, scoop out the flesh into a bowl, then blitz with a hand blender. Push the pulp through a sieve and mix with the lime zest and juice. Beat the sugar and egg yolks until pale, then beat in the cream and fruit juice. Carefully pour into the tart case, then bake for 40 minutes or until set with a very slight wobble. Remove from the oven, then leave to cool completely.

3 Serve the tart as it is, or dust the top with icing sugar and caramelize it using a blowtorch.

• Per slice 546 kcalories, protein 6g, carbohydrate 57g, fat 34g, saturated fat 13g, fibre 2g, sugar 34g, salt 0.36g

These cheeky Eccles mince pies are the perfect mid-afternoon treat, or a interesting alternative to mince pies at Christmas time. You don't even need a special tin to make them in.

Little Eccles pies

500g block all-butter puff pastry
flour, for dusting
450g/1lb mincemeat
1 egg white, lightly beaten
golden caster sugar, to sprinkle

Takes 30 minutes • Makes 18

1 Preheat the oven to 200°C/fan 180°C/ gas 6. Roll the pastry out on a floured surface to about the thickness of a 50p piece, then cut out 10cm/4in circles. Continue to re-roll and cut out until you have about 18 circles.
2 Place one teaspoon of mincemeat in the centre of each circle, brush the edges with egg white, then gather together tightly completely to encase the mincemeat.
3 Flip over the pies so the sealed edges are underneath, then squash them with your hand so you have a small, puck-shaped pie. Cut two small slits in the top of each pie, brush generously with egg white and scatter with sugar. Lift the pies on to baking sheets and bake for 15 minutes or until crisp and golden.

• Per pie 268 kcalories, protein 2g, carbohydrate 34g, fat 14g, saturated fat 3g, fibre 1g, sugar 22g, salt 0.27g

Make a sweet heart for your sweetheart – it doesn't matter if it's not Valentine's Day!

Treacle tart hearts

200g/8oz cold unsalted butter, cubed
350g/12oz plain flour, plus extra for rolling out
½ tsp ground ginger (optional)
100g/4oz golden caster sugar
1 egg yolk

FOR THE FILLING
400g/14oz golden syrup
zest of 1 lemon and juice of ½
100g/4oz white breadcrumbs

Takes 45 minutes • Makes 8

1 Blitz the butter, flour and ginger (if using) to fine crumbs in a food processor. Stir in the sugar. Add the egg yolk and two teaspoons of cold water. Pulse until the dough clumps together. Turn out on to a floured surface. Press into a round and chill for 30 minutes.
2 Roll the pastry to the thickness of two £1 coins and stamp out eight 11cm/4½in circles. Line eight 10cm-/4in-wide heart-shaped tins with pastry. Re-roll the trimmings and stamp out eight small hearts. Chill the tins and hearts for 15 minutes or until firm. Preheat the oven to 170°C/fan 150°C/gas 3. Put in a baking sheet.
3 Stir the syrup, lemon juice and zest together. Divide the breadcrumbs among the tins. Spoon over the syrup slowly. Top with the hearts. Put the tins on to the hot sheet. Bake for 25 minutes or until the pastry is golden. Cool for 15 minutes, then turn out on to a wire rack. Serve just warm.

• Per tart 452 kcalories, protein 5g, carbohydrate 78g, fat 16g, saturated fat 10g, fibre 2g, sugar 47g, salt 0.59g

Turn strawberries and cream into a pudding to remember with the simple addition of puff pastry sheets. Perfect for a sunny summer's day.

Strawberry and cream layer

375g block all-butter puff pastry
4 tbsp icing sugar
450g/14oz ripe strawberries, halved or quartered
1 vanilla pod or 1 tsp vanilla extract
284ml carton double cream
140g/5oz golden caster sugar

Takes 35 minutes • Serves 4

1 Preheat the oven to 220°C/fan 200°C/gas 7. Roll out the pastry to a 30cm/12in square. Lay it on a large baking sheet, place another sheet on top and bake for about 20 minutes or until golden.
2 Heat the grill to high, dust the pastry liberally with icing sugar and carefully caramelize under the grill. Dust with another layer of icing sugar and return to the grill to caramelize again. While warm, cut the pastry into 12 neat rectangles, trimming the edges as you go.
3 Dust the strawberries with a little icing sugar and set aside. Split the vanilla pod and scrape the seeds into the cream, then whip lightly with the caster sugar until it just holds its shape.
4 To assemble, place a blob of cream on each plate and stack the biscuits, cream and strawberries at jaunty angles.

• Per serving 931 kcalories, protein 7g, carbohydrate 96g, fat 60g, saturated fat 30g, fibre 1g, sugar 62g, salt 0.81g

Everyone loves good old fashioned apple pie, served just warm with cream or icecream.

Deep-filled Bramley apple pie

5 tbsp brandy
200g/8oz sultanas
plain flour for dusting
2 × 375g packs all-butter shortcrust pastry, squashed together
5 medium Bramley apples, peeled, cored and finely sliced
¼ tsp each ground cinnamon, nutmeg and allspice
140g/5oz golden caster sugar
1 egg, beaten with a splash of milk
vanilla ice cream or clotted cream, to serve

Takes 1 hour 10 minutes • Serves 8

1 Preheat the oven to 200°C/fan 180°C/gas 6. Heat sultanas with the brandy in the microwave until plump. Cut off one-third of the pastry, dust the surface with flour, then roll the rest into a large circle and use to line a 23cm/9in shallow, springform cake tin, overhanging the rim. Chill.
2 Toss the apples with the sultanas, spices and all but two tablespoons of sugar. Roll out the rest of the pastry, then cut it into a circle, using the base of the tin as a guide. Arrange the apple in the cake tin. Cover with the circle of pastry and tuck down the sides. Brush the lid with egg, then fold the overhanging pastry back over and pinch to seal. Brush with egg, slash the top and sprinkle with sugar.
3 Bake for 30–35 minutes or until golden. Cool for 1 hour, then run a knife around the pie's edge. Unclip the side of the tin and remove the pie.

• Per slice 646 kcalories, protein 8g, carbohydrate 93g, fat 27g, saturated fat 11g, fibre 4g, sugar 48g, salt 1g

Versions of this cake are eaten on Twelfth Night all over Europe. Buried inside each one is a trinket and whoever finds it is king for the day.

Cake of kings

85g/3oz candied citrus peel, chopped
100g/4oz raisins
50g/2oz pine nuts
50g/2oz glacé cherries
5 tbsp brandy
500g/1lb 2oz plain flour
3 tsp easy-blend yeast
1 tsp salt
150ml/¼pt milk, warmed
100g/4oz butter, softened
100g/4oz caster sugar
grated zest of 2 lemons and 1 orange
4 eggs, beaten
1 trinket or dried bean (in greaseproof paper)

TO FINISH
1 egg yolk, beaten with 1 tbsp water
175g/6oz candied fruits, sliced
6 sugar lumps, roughly crushed
apricot jam, to glaze

Takes about 4 hours, plus overnight soaking • Serves 20

1 Soak the peel, raisins, pine nuts and cherries in the brandy overnight. Mix 140g/5oz of the flour and the yeast in a bowl. Tip the remaining flour and salt into another bowl, make a well, then gradually beat in the milk to make a batter. Leave for 20 minutes or until frothy.

2 In another bowl, cream the butter, sugar and zests. Beat in the eggs gradually. Stir into the batter with remaining flour to make a dough. Knead on a floured surface for 5 minutes until smooth and elastic. Knead in the fruit mix. Put the dough in a clean bowl, cover. Leave for 2 hours until doubled in size.

3 Butter a baking sheet. Knead the dough briefly, then shape into a sausage about 50cm/20in long. Curl on to the sheet in a ring shape, pinching the ends together. Tuck the trinket under the cake, cover and leave for 1 hour or until doubled in size. Preheat the oven to 190°C/fan 170°C/gas 5.

4 Brush the cake with egg. Decorate with candied fruits and sugar. Bake for 45 minutes. Brush with jam then allow to cool before cutting.

• Per slice 252 kcalories, protein 5g, carbohydrate 41g, fat 8g, saturated fat 3g, fibre 1g, added sugar 13g, salt 0.43g

The filling in this South-African tart ends up like a gorgeous, sweet coconut macaroon. For an authentic touch, eat served with cups of Rooibos or redbush tea.

Coconut tart

½ tsp ground cinnamon
4 cardamom pods, shelled and seeds crushed
175g/6oz desiccated coconut
225g/8oz caster sugar
¾in × 500g block all-butter shortcrust pastry
plain flour, for dusting
1 egg, beaten
25g/1oz butter, melted
Cape gooseberries (physalis), to serve (optional)

Takes 1 hr 10 minutes • Serves 8

1 Preheat the oven to 200°C/fan 180°C/gas 6. Place a shallow 23cm/9in flan tin on a baking sheet. Tip the spices, coconut and sugar into a pan with 150ml/5fl oz water and cook over a low heat for about 5 minutes, stirring frequently to ensure the mixture doesn't catch. Set aside to cool.

2 Meanwhile, roll out the pastry on a lightly floured surface and use it to line the flan tin. Trim off the excess, fill the pastry case with baking parchment and baking beans and cook for 15 minutes. Remove the beans and cook for 5 minutes more.

3 Beat the egg and melted butter into the cooled coconut mixture, then spoon into the pastry case and smooth the top. Bake for 25 minutes or until the pastry is golden and the coconut a pale gold.

• Per slice 567 kcalories, protein 6g, carbohydrate 62g, fat 35g, saturated fat 20g, fibre 5g, sugar 32g, salt 0.73g

Adding banana to the custard gives a classic tart a new edge.

Banana custard tarts

500g block rich shortcrust pastry
plain flour, to dust
200ml/7fl oz full-fat milk
200ml/7fl oz double cream
3 eggs, plus 1 yolk
2 tbsp golden caster sugar
pinch of grated fresh nutmeg, plus
extra to serve
2 bananas, cut into chunks and
tossed in the juice of 1 lemon

Takes about 1 hour, plus chilling
Makes 6

1 Roll the pastry on a floured surface to the thickness of a 20p coin. Cut out six 15cm/6in circles of pastry. Use to line six tartlet tins, 9cm/3½ in diameter. Chill for 30 minutes.
2 Preheat the oven to 200°C/fan 180°C/ gas 6. Line each pastry case with non-stick baking paper, then fill with baking beans. Bake the pastry for 15 minutes then remove the paper and beans. Bake for another 5 minutes or until the pastry is light gold. Cool. Reduce the oven to 150°C/fan 130°C/gas 2.
3 Put the milk and cream into a pan and bring to the boil. Beat the eggs, egg yolk, sugar and nutmeg, then mix into the hot liquid. Divide the bananas among the cases, then fill with custard. Bake for 30 minutes until just set. Cool in the tins for 5 minutes before turning out on to a wire rack to cool. Finish with an extra grating of nutmeg.

• Per tart 703 kcalories, protein 11g, carbohydrate 57g, fat 50 g, saturated fat 21g, fibre 2g, sugar 23g, salt 0.59g

Keep a pack of puff pastry in the freezer and you'll always have a quick stand-by dessert – just use whatever fruit happens to be around or in season.

Creamy rhubarb tarts

375g block all-butter puff pastry
1 egg, beaten
1 tbsp demerara sugar
1 tbsp crème fraîche
2 sticks rhubarb, thinly sliced on an angle
2 tbsp icing sugar

Takes 50 minutes • Makes 4

1 Preheat the oven to 220°C/fan 200°C/gas 7. Roll the pastry out thinly then cut out four circles about 15cm/6in diameter. Use a slightly smaller cutter to cut a circle out of the middle and trim away the outside border, reserving these trimmings. Lay the four circles on a baking sheet, prick with a fork and brush the edges with egg. Use the pastry trimmings to make a border around the edge (like a vol-au-vent) and press down gently. Chill.
2 In a small bowl, mix the demerara sugar with the crème fraîche, then spread a thin amount over the base of each tart. Arrange slices of rhubarb over the crème fraîche, then dust generously with icing sugar. Bake for 20 minutes or until puffed and golden.

• Per tart 433 kcalories, protein 8g, carbohydrate 44g, fat 28g, saturated fat 18g, fibre 3g, sugar 14g, salt 0.54g

The perfect addition to an afternoon cup of tea, this zingy citrus pie uses ginger nut biscuits for the base so there's no need to worry about making pastry.

Biscuity lime pie

300g pack ginger nut biscuits
100g/4oz butter, melted
3 egg yolks
50g/2oz golden caster sugar
zest and juice of 4 limes, plus lime slices (optional), to serve
zest and juice of 1 lemon
397g can sweetened condensed milk

Takes 1 hour • Serves 6

1 Preheat the oven to 180°C/fan 160°C/gas 4. Tip the biscuits into a food processor and blitz to crumbs. Pulse in the butter. Tip into a fluted tart tin, about 10x34cm/4x13in (or a 20cm/8in round tin) and press into the base and up the sides. Bake for 15 minutes until crisp.

2 Tip the egg yolks, sugar, lime and lemon zests into a bowl and beat with an electric hand whisk until doubled in volume. Pour in the condensed milk, beat until combined, then add the citrus juices.

3 Pour the mix into the tart case and bake for 20 minutes or until just set with a slight wobble in the centre. Leave to set completely, then remove from the tin, cool and chill. Serve in slices topped with thin lime slices, if you like.

• Per slice 633 kcalories, protein 10g, carbohydrate 85g, fat 30g, saturated fat 15g, fibre 1g, sugar 64g, salt 0.93g

Custard made with caramel gives this tart a wonderful toffee-apple flavour.

Caramel custard apple tart

375g block dessert pastry
140g/5oz golden caster sugar
8 eating apples, peeled, cored and cut into wedges
splash of apple brandy (optional)
284ml carton double cream
4 egg yolks, beaten in a large bowl

Takes 1 hour 25 minutes • Serves 8

1 Preheat the oven to 220°C/fan 200°C/gas 7. Roll the pastry on a floured surface to about a £1 coin thickness. Use to line a deep 23cm/9in tart tin, leaving an overhang. Line with non-stick baking paper and baking beans, then bake for 15 minutes until the edges are golden. Remove the beans and cook for 5 minutes more until golden brown. Cool. Reduce the oven to 160°C/fan 140°C/gas 3.

2 Meanwhile, heat the sugar in a large frying pan until it dissolves and caramelizes. Carefully tip in the apple wedges and toss well. Splash in the brandy, if using, then cook for 2–3 minutes or until just starting to soften, then take off the heat.

3 Pour the cream into the juices in the pan then whisk into the yolks. Using a slotted spoon, arrange the apple wedges over the tart base, pour over the custard, then bake for 40 minutes or until just set. Once cooled, cut away the spare pastry and neaten the edges.

• Per slice 556 kcalories, protein 5g, carbohydrate 54g, fat 37g, saturated fat 17g, fibre 3g, sugar 36g, salt 0.28g

The pastry cream that fills this tart is easy to make, as the little bit of flour holds it all together without danger of it turning into scrambled egg.

Strawberry vanilla tart

250g/9oz block of sweet shortcrust pastry

FOR THE CRÈME PÂTISSIÈRE
5 egg yolks
2 tsp vanilla sugar
100g/4oz caster sugar
50g/2oz plain flour
425ml/¾ pint milk
25g/1oz butter

TO FINISH
500g/1lb 2oz strawberries (preferably small), halved
2 tbsp redcurrant or quince jelly, warmed with 1 tbsp water

Takes 1 hour, plus cooling • Serves 8

1 Preheat the oven to 190°C/fan 170°C/gas 5. Roll out the pastry and use to line a shallow 23cm/9in tart tin. Cover the pastry with non-stick baking paper and a layer of baking beans. Bake blind for 10 minutes, then remove the beans and paper, and bake for 10 minutes or until crisp and golden. Remove from the tin and cool on a wire rack.
2 Whisk the egg yolks, vanilla and sugars until pale and thick. Whisk in the flour.
3 Boil the milk, then gradually whisk into the egg mixture. Return to the pan and cook gently, whisking, until thickened and glossy. Cook gently for 2 minutes then beat in the butter. Spoon into a clean bowl, cover the surface with cling film and let it cool.
4 Fill the tart case with custard and arrange the strawberries on top. Brush the warm jelly glaze over the strawberries to finish.

• Per slice 345 kcalories, protein 6g, carbohydrate 43g, fat 17g, saturated fat 6g, fibre 1g, sugar 26g, salt 0.30g

Adding apricots gives a modern twist to this classic French tart, while also making it lighter.

Apricot gâteau Pithiviers

100g/4oz butter, softened
140g/5oz golden caster sugar
1 egg, plus 1 egg yolk
100g/4oz ground almonds
1 tbsp plain flour
1 tbsp Grand Marnier or Disaronno
200g/8oz ripe apricots, stoned and thickly sliced

FOR THE PASTRY CASE
500g pack ready-made puff pastry
1 egg, beaten
3 tbsp apricot jam, melted and sieved

Takes 1 hour, plus chilling • Serves 10

1 Beat the butter, sugar, egg and yolk, almonds, flour and liqueur until smooth. Preheat the oven to 200°C/fan 180°C/gas 6. Roll out half the pastry to the thickness of two £1 coins, then cut a circle about 25cm/10in diameter. Roll out the remaining pastry and cut a second circle, slightly larger than the first.
2 Place the smaller circle on a baking sheet and top with half the almond filling, then the apricots, then the rest of the filling, leaving a 2.5cm/1in border. Brush the border with egg and set the remaining pastry on top, pressing the edges firmly together.
3 With a sharp knife, score lines around the outer edge of the pastry. Press the back of the knife 1cm/½in into the edge at regular intervals to give a scalloped appearance. Brush the top with more beaten egg then score radiating curved lines. Chill for 20 minutes.
4 Bake for 30–35 minutes until puffed and golden. Leave to cool then glaze with the jam.

• Per slice 429 kcalories, protein 7g, carbohydrate 40g, fat 28g, saturated fat 11g, fibre 1g, added sugar 17g, salt 0.60g

This recipe also works well with plums, but halve the amount of sugar you use as plums are a lot sweeter.

Flip-over damson pie

500g/1lb 2oz damsons, halved
and stoned
140g/5oz golden caster sugar
pinch of ground cinnamon
425g pack (2 sheets) ready-rolled
puff pastry
1 egg, beaten
icing sugar, to dust

Takes 40 minutes • Serves 4

1 Preheat the oven to 220°C/fan 200°C/ gas 7. Mix the damsons, sugar and cinnamon together in a bowl. Lay one pastry sheet on a baking sheet, and pile the damsons down the middle, leaving space around the edge. Brush the edges with egg then drape over the other sheet of pastry. Trim the edge of the pie and press down to seal.

2 Brush the pie with egg and make a series of parallel slits across it, avoiding the edges. Bake for 30 minutes or until puffed up and golden. Leave to stand for a few minutes, dust with icing sugar, slice and serve with custard.

• Per slice 605 kcalories, protein 9g, carbohydrate 88g, fat 27g, saturated fat 10g, fibre 2g, added sugar 36g, salt 0.9g

Mixing and kneading this classic bread in the food processor means that you can make a very soft dough very easily. It will keep for 2 days and is delicious, at any time, spread with apricot jam.

Easy Easter brioche

250g/9oz plain flour, plus extra for rolling
100g/4oz butter, cut into small pieces
2 rounded tbsp caster sugar
good pinch of salt
7g sachet easy-blend dried yeast
3 eggs
beaten egg yolk, to glaze
2–3 sugar cubes, lightly crushed

Takes 2¾ hours • Serves 6

1 Tip the flour into a food processor fitted with a plastic kneading blade. Add the butter. Process until the mixture looks like breadcrumbs. Stir in sugar, salt and yeast.
2 Add the eggs and mix to a soft dough, then knead in the machine for 2 minutes. Butter a brioche mould or 900g/2lb loaf tin. Tip the dough out on to a lightly floured surface and then, with floured hands, knead very briefly to form a ball. Drop the dough into the tin, smooth side up. Cover with oiled cling film and leave in a warm place for about 2 hours or until doubled in size.
3 Heat the oven to 200°C/fan 180°C/gas 6. Brush the top of the brioche with egg yolk, then sprinkle over the crushed sugar and bake for 20–25 minutes or until golden brown and the bottom of the loaf sounds hollow when tapped. Cool on a wire rack.

• Per slice 365 kcalories, protein 9g, carbohydrate 43g, fat 19g, saturated fat 10g, fibre 1g, sugar 11g, salt 0.71g

These appealing little slices make a lighter, really fruity alternative to mince pies.

Chunky mince pie slices

280g/10oz mincemeat
25g/1oz pecan nuts, mix of broken and whole
25g/1oz pistachio nuts, halved lengthways
2 tbsp flaked almonds
25g/1oz dried cranberries
½ small apple, peeled cored and finely chopped
finely grated zest of 1 lemon, plus 2 tsp of juice
375g ready-rolled sheet puff pastry
1 rounded tbsp ground almonds
50g/2oz icing sugar

Takes 35 minutes • Makes 15

1 Preheat the oven to 220°C/fan 200°C/gas 7. Combine the mincemeat with the nuts, cranberries, apple and lemon zest.
2 Unroll the pastry on to a floured work surface. Slice off a strip across one end to leave a 23cm/9in square of pastry. Cut out 15–30 star shapes from the strip, thinly re-rolling the trimmings until it is all used up.
3 Lay the pastry square on a baking sheet and scatter over the ground almonds. Spread the mincemeat mixture over so that it comes right to the edge of the pastry. Lay the stars in lines across the mincemeat, slightly overlapping them to fit, if necessary, so that you can cut out 15 slices when baked.
4 Bake for 15 minutes or until the pastry is golden. Leave to cool. Mix the icing sugar with two teaspoons of lemon juice. Drizzle over the cool pastry and cut into 15 slices.

• Per slice 204 kcalories, protein 3g, carbohydrate 27g, fat 10g, saturated fat 3g, fibre 1g, sugar 17g, salt 0.21g

The ultimate sticky, spicy bun for teatime, and so much better than bought. To serve, simply split and butter them or toast until golden.

Richly fruited hot cross buns

500g pack white bread mix
50g/2oz caster sugar
1 tbsp mixed spice
85g/3oz butter, melted
250ml/9fl oz milk, warmed
1 egg, beaten
250g bag mixed fruit (including peel)

TO DECORATE
100g/4oz plain flour, plus extra
for dusting
2 tbsp golden syrup or honey,
to glaze

Takes 50 minutes, plus rising time
Makes 12

1 Combine the bread mix, sugar and spice in a bowl, and make a well in the centre. Tip the butter, milk and egg into the well, and mix to a soft dough. Knead on a lightly floured surface for about 5 minutes or until smooth. Transfer to a lightly oiled bowl, cover with oiled cling film and leave until doubled in size.
2 Knead briefly then press out into a large rectangle. Sprinkle the fruit over, then roll the dough up around the fruit and knead until evenly dispersed. Split into 12 even-sized balls.
3 Transfer the buns to a large greased baking sheet, 2–3cm/¾–1in apart. Cover and leave until risen and pillowy.
4 Preheat the oven to 200°C/fan 180°C/gas 6. Whisk six tablespoons of water into the flour until smooth. Spoon the mixture into a freezer bag, snip off the end and 'pipe' across the buns. Bake for 15–20 minutes or until risen and golden. Cool for a few minutes, then lift on to a wire rack. Heat the syrup then brush over the warm buns.

• Per bun 300 kcalories, protein 7g, carbohydrate 52g, fat 9g, saturated fat 4g, fibre 3g, added sugar 23g, salt 1.16g

These luxurious mince pies have a tempting almond layer hidden under the short, crumbly crust.

Deep-filled mince pies

900g/2lb mincemeat

FOR THE PASTRY
400g/14oz butter, very cold, cut into cubes
700g/1lb 8oz plain flour, plus extra for rolling out
200g/8oz golden caster sugar
¼ tsp salt
2 egg yolks

FOR THE ALMOND FILLING
200g/8oz ground almonds
200g/8oz golden caster sugar
4 egg whites
few drops of almond extract
1 egg, beaten, to seal and glaze

Takes 45 minutes • Makes 20–24

1 To make the pastry, rub the butter and flour together to form fine crumbs, stir in the sugar and salt, then add the egg yolks, one tablespoon of water and mix. Press into a ball, split in two and knead each half briefly until smooth. Wrap in cling film and chill.
2 Preheat the oven to 200°C/fan 180°C/ gas 6. Beat together the almonds, sugar, egg whites and almond extract. Roll out a ball of pastry on a lightly floured surface and cut out twelve 10cm/4in circles. Push into the wells of a muffin tin. Re-roll the leftover pastry and cut out twelve 8cm/3in circles for the tops.
3 Spoon one heaped tablespoon of mincemeat into each case, followed by one tablespoon of almond mix. Brush the edges with egg, press on the tops and brush with egg too. Bake for 20 minutes until golden. Cool for 10 minutes in the tin then lift out. Repeat with the rest of the pastry and fillings.

• Per pie (for 24) 546 kcalories, protein 7g, carbohydrate 77g, fat 25g, saturated fat 12g, fibre 2g, sugar 50g, salt 0.39g

Based on the old, classic recipe for Chelsea buns, these whirls smell so heavenly that no one will be able to resist. The banana and apricot filling is a hit with children too.

Banana and cinnamon whirls

100g/4oz strong white flour, plus extra for dusting
100g/4oz malted granary bread flour
½ tsp salt
7g sachet easy-blend dried yeast
5 tbsp warm milk
1 egg, beaten
3–5 tbsp warm water
25g/1oz unsalted butter, melted
2 medium bananas, thinly sliced
100g/4oz dried apricots, chopped
50g/2oz light muscovado sugar
1 tsp ground cinnamon
zest of ½ orange
2 tbsp clear honey, warmed

Takes 40 minutes, plus rising time
Makes 9

1 Mix the flours, salt and yeast in a large bowl and make a well in the centre. Pour in the milk, egg and enough of the water to form a soft dough. Dust the surface with flour, knead for 5 minutes or until smooth, then leave in an oiled bowl, covered with cling film, until doubled in size.
2 Lightly butter a 20cm/8in square tin. On a floured surface, roll the dough into a large rectangle (30x25cm/12x10in) and brush with butter.
3 Mix together the fruit, sugar, cinnamon and zest, then spread it over the dough, leaving a border. Roll up from the long side then press the ends to seal. Cut into nine pieces and place in the tin cut side up, just touching. Cover and leave to rise for 30 minutes.
4 Heat the oven to 200°C/fan 180°C/ gas 6. Brush half the honey over the buns. Bake for 20–25 minutes or until golden. Cool for 10 minutes before removing to a wire rack. Brush with the remaining honey.

• Per whirl 191 kcalories, protein 5g, carbohydrate 36g, fat 4g, saturated fat 2g, fibre 2g, sugar 18g, salt 0.32g

Index

Picture credits and recipe credits

BBC *Good Food* magazine and BBC Books would like to thank the following people for providing photos. While every effort has been made to trace and acknowledge all photographers, we should like to apologize should there be any errors or omissions.

Marie-Louise Avery p75; Steve Baxter p157; Peter Cassidy p11, p38, p125, p177; Jean Cazals p81, p115, p135, p173, p178, p189, p193, p199; William Lingwood p29, p167; Gareth Morgans p21, p67, p73, p79; David Munns p13, p25, p57, p93, p107, p111, p131, p149, p163, p171, p185, p203; Myles New p17, p47, p51, p77, p83, p87, p117, p139, p147, p151, p155, p159, p161, p165, 209; Lis Parsons p15, p19, p31, p33, p35, p43, p53, p55, p63, p95, p109, p119, p145, p207; Craig Robertson p65, p85; Roger Stowell p103, p197; Debbie Treloar p137; Simon Walton p23, p205; Cameron Watt p153; Philip Webb p6, p27, p37, p41, p45, p49, p59, p61, p69, p71, p91, p101, p105, p113, p121, p123, p127, p133, p141, p143, p169, p183, p187, p191, p195, p201; Simon Wheeler p97, p99, p129; Kate Whitaker p89, p175, p181; Elizabeth Zeschin p211

All the recipes in this book were created by the editorial team at *Good Food* and by regular contributors to the magazine.